LOVE YOUR WINE

LOVE YOUR WINE

GET TO GRIPS
WITH WHAT YOU'RE DRINKING

Cathy Marston

BOOKSTORM

ISBN: 978-1-920434-83-0
e-ISBN: 978-1-920434-84-7

First edition, first impression 2014

Published by Bookstorm (Pty) Ltd
PO Box 4532, Northcliff 2115, Johannesburg, South Africa
www.bookstorm.co.za

Distributed by On the Dot
www.onthedot.co.za

Edited by Mark Ronan
Proofread by Wesley Thompson
Cover design by Karin Barry
Photographs supplied by various contributors
Book design and typesetting by René de Wet
Printed by Creda Communications, Cape Town

I RAISE A GLASS TO MY PARENTS, WHO HAVE WAITED A LONG TIME FOR THIS – I HOPE THEY THINK IT'S WORTH IT. AND TO KEVIN AND CHARLIE, BOTH OF WHOM ARE BETTER SABRAGEURS THAN ME, THANKS FOR ALL YOUR PATIENCE AND LOVE.

CONTENTS

INTRODUCTION

Wine is easy. No, really, it is. Wine is something you grow and you turn it into something you drink. Look at it this way: bread is something you grow and you turn it into something you eat, but you don't see people in the baked-goods aisle of a supermarket flummoxed by the range of products or agonising over their choice, do you? No one gets confused by wholemeal bread, wholegrain, best of both, white, rye, pumpernickel, brown, seed ... Well, maybe they do, but you know what I mean. If you have enough confidence to buy a loaf of bread, then you should be confident enough to buy a bottle of wine.

And that is precisely what this book wants to do – give you confidence about wine.

'I DON'T KNOW ANYTHING ABOUT WINE, BUT I KNOW WHAT I LIKE'

This book aims to give you the confidence to believe that you know more than some superior waiter trying to patronise you and con you into paying more than you're comfortable with; the confidence to ask the right sorts of questions, so you can learn what you really want to know about the wines you buy; and, most of all, the confidence to enjoy drinking wine, to see it as a pleasure, not a potential source of embarrassment.

Am I going to get all that from one small book? I see you asking yourself as you search for the secret 'button of success' on the spine. Well, hopefully you'll come close. And if you don't, keep trying because the real secret of success in wine is that the more you drink, the more you know. (Admittedly, the less you will probably remember but, hey, you can't have everything.)

Treat this book like a swimming pool – dip your toes in to test the water, leap in from any point that takes your fancy, splash about, enjoy yourself, then when you're exhausted, lie down in the sunshine and sip a glass of something delicious.

1

HOW TO USE THIS BOOK

WELL, IT'S GOOD FOR WEDGING OPEN DOORS, SWATTING FLIES, PROPPING UP WOBBLY RESTAURANT TABLES – AND YOU MAY EVEN WANT TO READ BITS OF IT AS WELL. I SAY 'BITS', BECAUSE I REALLY DON'T MIND IF YOU DON'T READ IT ALL.

Some of you may already be eager, curious, adventurous drinkers who are greedy to find out more about your favourite tipple, and will hopefully find lots of answers and starting points among these august pages. On the other hand, some of you may have very little interest beyond drinking the wine that you already enjoy – and that's also fine. When it comes to wine, there are far too many snobs, experts, fundis and taste-autocrats, all of whom will lecture you on what you should be drinking, rather than helping you get the most out of the wines you enjoy. Sure, if you're looking for something new, then this book can also help you with your search, but if you like drinking simple, uncomplicated, everyday wines and see no need to change, then neither do I.

So this book is structured as a kind of ladder to wine drinking. No one is saying you have to start at the bottom rung; but no one is saying you have to reach the top one either. There are eleven chapters that are named after certain styles of wine, so whichever style you currently enjoy, this should be your starting point. You may want to go back and read the previous chapters to see if there's anything you didn't already know or that you might find interesting. Or you may be eager to find out about some styles you are unfamiliar with – in which case, read ahead, it's up to you. So, start where you feel comfortable and stop when you're happy with what you're drinking – you can always come back later to find out more.

These chapters are quite brief because they may be a little bit technical – not much, but maybe a little. If you're the kind of person who doesn't want to know what they're drinking beyond the fact that it says 'wine' on the label, feel free to ignore these sections. On the other hand, they do contain useful and interesting information that will stand you in excellent stead at a school fundraising quiz night or when you want to show off your knowledge to a snotty sommelier or other expert.

These chapters are intended as snippets to explain winemaking know-how in steps, rather than giving you all the information at the beginning, freaking you out and sending you shrieking away from the wine aisles in horror and desperation. Each 'wine tech' will add a little more information each time, taking you to the next step on the wine 'ladder'. Read them or don't read them. As you like.

I have the attention span of a gnat – oh look, a puppy – so I've included interviews with some professionals to vary the tone and give you some insight provided by people in South Africa's wine industry. We have so many fascinating, charismatic, passionate and interesting wine folk in South Africa, it seems a shame not to give them a bit of space where they can tell you what they think about wine. Plus, it was a good excuse to sit and chat with them, and drink. Score.

WINE RECOMMENDATIONS

In each chapter, I've suggested a few wines that you may want to try in sections called 'Try these'. Most of them should be readily available, but if you can't find them ask your retailer to suggest something similar. The suggestions are intended to be the next-step wines, so they probably won't be the old favourites you're already drinking but, hopefully, they will help broaden your taste horizons without scaring you back into the arms of your tried-and-tested tipples – it's all about baby steps here.

Wines are best enjoyed with friends, so don't make a big fuss about trying these wines in a formal kind of tasting set-up. Just take a second or two for that first sip, think about the flavours, think about things like sugar levels, acid levels, tannins (don't panic – there will be explanations of all these and more later). Then swallow, have one more 30-second think about whether you actually like this wine (always the most important consideration) and if you do, then fill your glass and enjoy.

FOOD AND WINE MATCHES

I know a lot of people who believe that everything is better with bacon but, personally, I believe everything is better with wine. Not that I get hung up on perfect food–wine pairings or anything – in fact, quite the opposite. I think that the wine you enjoy will always taste better with food than the wine that you're TOLD is a good match, so you must drink it. Because everyone is different, no one's palate works quite the same way and despite the best efforts of all food-and-wine-matching Nazis, if you don't drink red wine, then you just don't drink red wine.

So I've made a few suggestions and given you a couple of things to think about if you want to try match some food with some wines. But, in general, be confident with your choices and don't think too hard about it because most wine kind of goes with most food. And that's the secret truth nobody else will tell you, except me.

Finally, there is a glossary of wine-related terms at the back of the book that you can use to impress people, or to remind yourself of the meanings of some of the (very few) technical words you'll find as you read.

So that's it. Treat this book like a swimming pool – dip your toes in to test the water, leap in from any point that takes your fancy, splash about, enjoy yourself, then when you're exhausted, lie down in the sunshine and sip a glass of something delicious.

If you've got a question and can't find the answer, then feel free to ask me directly. You can find me on social media or via the website www.thewinecentre.co.za. The only stupid question is the one you don't ask, so get in touch and tell me what's on your mind. I'll be sipping – I mean sitting – waiting for your call. ☺

PS – it's worth mentioning that what I'm telling you about winemaking in this book is the 'normal' way things happen in the wine world. Sure, you may come across a winemaker who does the opposite to what I've described, because there are exceptions to everything and nothing more so than in the world of wine. This book tells you what *generally* happens, so please don't waste your time and mine by telling me I'm wrong and that so-and-so applies a winemaking process differently. I know this already, and your time would be much better spent chilling out and drinking more wine.

The wine is bottled and a label stuck on it, and then you and I, dear reader, spend our hard-earned cash buying it, drinking it and hopefully enjoying it. And that is it. Winemaking 101 in a nutshell. You can stop reading now – you know everything.

2

Wine tech **NO. 1**

THE ABSOLUTE BASICS OF WINEMAKING
(THE MINIMUM YOU NEED TO KNOW)

I KNOW I SAID THAT YOU DON'T NEED TO READ THE 'WINE TECH' SECTIONS
OF THIS BOOK, BUT IF YOU CAN POSSIBLY SCREW UP THE COURAGE TO
TRY JUST ONE OF THEM, THIS IS THE ONE TO READ. 'CAUSE IT WILL BE
USEFUL, I PROMISE.

Okay – first things first. Wine is made from grapes. I know that there's rice wine and elderberry wine etc., but let's not go there right now okay? Wine is made from grapes – full stop. These are not the same as the table grapes you get at the supermarket, but a whole load of individual grape varieties specially 'bred' over the years for making wine, and they all have different flavours and characteristics. It's kind of like apples – think of a tart Granny Smith, a crunchy Golden Delicious, a sweet Pink Lady – different flavours and textures, but they're all still apples. And that's how grapes are too.

So, wine is made from grapes, and grapes are a fruit. We don't eat fruit when it's not ripe: we wait until the sun has done its job, ripened the grapes and created lovely, juicy, sweet flavours. Then we pick the fruit, crush the fruit and make sweet, sticky juice.

Now, here's the most important thing you need to know about wine. The equation that makes sense of it all and the only bit of really technical stuff you're going to get in the whole book:

Sugar + Yeast
= Alcohol + Carbon Dioxide

I'll say that again – sugar plus yeast equals alcohol and carbon dioxide (seems far friendlier when I write it like that). This equation describes what happens during fermentation, and it is pretty much the same process that takes place in the making of beer, cider, nail-polish remover or any other form of alcohol you care to name.

In fact, the equation will allow you to work out quite a few things about wine yourself – what the equation is saying is that if grapes are grown in a hot area, they will be riper and sweeter. Think about it – the kinds of fruits grown in hot parts of the world (e.g. pineapples, mangoes, granadillas and the like) are much sweeter than those that grow in cooler areas, where you find things like apples and pears. So, in hotter areas, the sugar levels in the fruit are higher, whereas the acidity (that tart taste you notice when you eat an under-ripe fruit) is lower. The higher levels of sugar will then produce higher levels of alcohol (because sugar + yeast = alcohol + carbon dioxide), which makes the wines seem richer and more full-bodied. And that, in a nutshell, is why wines grown in different regions are different.

So if the grapes are grown in a hotter area, then expect:
- more alcohol
- more body
- and probably less acidity.

If they are from a cooler area, then you should find:

- less alcohol
- lighter, more refreshing wines
- and generally higher acidity.

It may also come as no surprise that most of the warmer areas make more red wines, while cooler areas tend to produce more white wines. This is because – along with sugar – colour and tannin levels also increase in the grapes with sunshine and warmth. More on tannins in Chapter 10.

HOTTER WINE REGIONS OF SOUTH AFRICA

Generally, the hotter areas are inland, where the vineyards aren't exposed to the effect of cooling sea breezes:

- Calitzdorp
- Paarl
- Robertson
- Swartland
- Tulbagh
- Wellington
- Worcester
- Orange River (Northern Cape)

Sea breezes affect these vineyards and keep the grapes nice and cool, allowing them to take their time to ripen fully:

((() Constantia

((() Darling

((() Durbanville

((() Elgin

((() Hemel-en-Aarde

The Elgin region is cool not because it is close to the sea, but because it is quite elevated and the microclimate is cooler than in the lower-lying areas. Other regions, such as Stellenbosch and Franschhoek, are neither entirely hot nor cool but have different pockets in both areas.

BACK TO WINEMAKING!

Anyway, so you've squeezed out your grape juice and added yeast – not quite the same strains of yeast as those you use to make your morning loaf, but of the same family. The yeast feeds on the sugars like a hungry teenager after a night on the town and converts them into alcohol, at the same time farting off copious amounts of CO_2 (a reminder of the fermentation equation again: sugar + yeast = alcohol + CO_2 – I'll be testing you on this later).

After the yeast has done its work, the winemaker may decide to do a few other bits and pieces to it (which we'll come to later on in the book), then the wine is cleaned up by removing anything unsightly or murky left over from fermentation. The wine is bottled and a label stuck on it, and then you and I, dear reader, spend our hard-earned cash buying it, drinking it and hopefully enjoying it.

And that is it. Winemaking 101 in a nutshell. You can stop reading now – you know everything. Okay, I may be joking a bit but honestly, that is pretty much it in terms of winemaking. I told you it wasn't much trickier than bread.

Going with the winemaking flow

with Ntsiki Biyela of Stellekaya Winery

You never know when the love of wine is going to hit you between the eyes and hook you forever. Ntsiki Biyela, winemaker at Stellekaya, in Stellenbosch, had planned an entirely different career path for herself when she was suddenly offered a scholarship to learn how to make wine. Until that point, she had had no contact with grapes apart from in a fruit salad, but over her four years at Stellenbosch University, she gradually came to realise how fascinating and challenging it is to make the perfect wine.

So what does it take to make this perfect wine? In Ntsiki's opinion, there are two crucial periods, 'harvest time and blending – those are the keys to the final bottle', and although she says she still follows the basic winemaking steps in the flow diagram taught to her in college, she now relies more on experience and instinct to craft her robust and warming red wines. Her winemaking activities aren't limited to South Africa either: she's made wine in Bordeaux, in France; in Italy; and the next country on her hit list is Israel. She also hopes to work in Burgundy at some point too. If she could just keep making the stuff and travelling and selling it, she'd be a happy woman, but the problems of officialdom always intrude: 'Worst thing for me about making wine? The administration that has to be done for every single drop,' she moans ruefully.

If winemaking hadn't been Ntsiki's original choice of career, it would be now, and she is a big advocate of encouraging others to consider the profession. She is a mentor and board member of the newly established Pinotage Youth Development Academy, which trains and supports young people seeking to work in all aspects of the wine industry. Her advice to others considering a future making wine? 'If you are in it for the money, don't bother, but if it is for satisfaction, for love and to earn a living, then it's a good place to be.' Would she choose winemaking if she had her life over again? 'Hell, yes!' she says. 'I don't feel I've made my best wine of my life yet, and with each year being different, it is exciting knowing that my best wine is yet to come.'

These are the sorts of wines that most people are snobby about

('Oh God, you mean you actually *like* that cheap, sweet crap?') and

I bet that many of you who drink them find yourselves apologising

for your wine choices to these taste Nazis. Stop that, stop it at once.

3

SWEET AND SEMI-SWEET WHITE WINES

AT THE RISK OF SOUNDING LIKE SOMETHING YOU MIGHT READ IN A WEIRD MAGAZINE ARTICLE, HAVE YOU EVER TRIED BREAST MILK? I BET MOST MOTHERS OUT THERE HAVE CAUGHT A DROP FROM TIME TO TIME AND IF YOU DO ACCIDENTALLY TASTE SOME, YOU'LL DISCOVER IT'S SWEET.

As human beings, we are actually programmed to like sweet things (it's something to do with the sugar giving us enough energy to go and forage for more food), and chances are that, as a baby, you graduated from milk to sweet food like puréed apples and pears, mashed butternut and sweet potato.

It's much the same when it comes to wine. Most of us start on sweet, semi-sweet or off-dry wine styles, simply because they're easier for us to accept and drink. I'm from the UK, so I cut my vinous teeth on semi-sweet German Riesling called Liebfraumilch, but many South Africans' first experiences of wine are products such as Van Loveren's Four Cousins, The Saints range or Robertson Winery. These tend to be low in price, often come in big bottles or boxes and are lower in alcohol. And they're all very – sometimes worryingly – easy to drink.

These are the sorts of wines that most people are snobby about ('Oh God, you mean you actually *like* that cheap, sweet crap?') and I bet that many of you who drink them find yourselves apologising for your wine choices to these taste Nazis. Stop that, stop it at once: when it comes to wine – in fact, when it comes to life – your motto should be 'never explain, never apologise'. And when their gums swell up from an excess of acidic Sauvignon Blanc, who's going to have the last laugh then, eh?

EVERYONE NEEDS A BIT OF BALANCE

To be fair to the wine snobs, a lot of what makes them despise these sweeter wines is that they often lack balance. What do I mean by that? When you put wine in your mouth, you should taste an even combination of sweet, sour, acid and fruit (we'll add more factors to this list later on). Often, these sweet and semi-sweet wines are so big on the sugar stakes that they are not offset by any of the other factors, and the result can be a wine that is cloyingly sweet or almost sticky in your mouth. If you want syrup, then drink syrup, but if you want a balanced wine you should look for one with a pleasing sweetness, some nice fruit flavours and a refreshing clean finish to it. That's what we mean by 'balance'.

HOW IS A WINE MADE SWEET?

The answer is simple: by leaving sugar in the wine. Some people refer to this as residual sugar (or RS) but whatever you call it, it's sweet. Depending on how the wine is made, the winemaker may either stop the fermentation before the yeast has chowed all the sugar (they can do this by filtering out the yeast) or by adding the sweetness afterwards by mixing in some sweet grape juice.

Here are a few favourites that offer a slightly less sweet alternative to some of the really sugary ones in big bottles or boxes.

EDGEBASTON THE BERRY BOX WHITE

This is a blend of Sauvignon Blanc, Semillon and Viognier, and has a lovely, lively hint of sweetness to the finish. Just off-dry, it's a refreshing drink, perfect for loading up with a few ice blocks on a hot day.

LANDSKROON OFF-DRY CHENIN BLANC

Isn't life easier when they actually tell you what style of wine is in the bottle? Fresh and fruity with lots of interest balancing out the moderate sweetness.

VAN LOVEREN NEIL'S PICK COLOMBAR

No need to leave the familiar Four Cousins family, just move up to this for a change. One of my absolute fave off-dry gluggers.

Perhaps unsurprisingly, many of the best food matches for sweet wines are slightly sweet foods. But not always. In fact, if a food is too sweet, it can have the effect of making your wine seem dry and bitter, which is not good. If you're pairing a dessert with a sweet or off-dry wine (but not a full-on dessert wine – see Chapter 18 for more on these styles), then as a very general rule, you'll be better off with light, fruity puddings than a sticky, soggy, chocolate fondant. If I were you, I'd go to the other extreme and find something spicy and aromatic. Food flavoured with hot chilli, fragrant curries, spicy rubs and marinades – all of these are calmed down by a semi-sweet or off-dry wine. It's always a matter of huge surprise to me that so many Asian restaurants don't have more off-dry offerings on their wine lists. Big mistake, I'd say – try it for yourself and see if I'm not right.

Thinking dry, drinking sweet

with Danelle Conradie of Van Loveren

Perhaps they won't always admit it, but a lot of winemakers started out on their drinking careers with sweeter styles of wine. One who has no hang-ups about her wine-drinking roots is Danelle Conradie, winemaker at Van Loveren. Danelle's drinking career began courtesy of her father, who enjoyed an off-dry wine from Twee Jonge Gezellen called Schanderl, which was a blend of Gewürztraminer, Riesling and Muscat – all aromatic varieties that do well as off-dry or semi-sweet wines, and so this was Danelle's first choice when she started buying wine for herself.

Danelle mainly crafts the premium range at Van Loveren, although the first time I met her was when she was a finalist at the Woman Winemaker of the Year competition with her amazing-value off-dry Colombar (which I included in the wine suggestions above) standing proudly alongside wines that were literally ten times the price. 'There is nothing less intrinsically superior about these off-dry and semi-sweet styles of wines. It's all to do with the complexity and character of the wine,' she says. Van Loveren's wines are probably the first steps to wine drinking for many thousands of South Africans via the hugely popular

Four Cousins range. The combination of big bottles, excellent prices and easy, fruity, uncomplicated crowd-pleasing wines makes for a brand that is currently the biggest-selling bottled wine in South Africa, and Danelle relishes seeing the pleasure on faces when they try her wines for the first time: 'Seeing people fall in love with wine because of Four Cousins is tremendously rewarding!'

When I chatted to her about sweeter-style wines, she pointed out something that I also believe to be true, namely that 'a lot of people talk "dry" but, actually, they drink sweet!' Because sweeter styles of wine are viewed so disparagingly by many, I often see that people ask for dry wines and then find them bitter or just 'too dry'. Offer them off-dry and you'll find they are much happier, even though they don't realise that it is the spoonful of sugar that is helping this particularly delicious medicine go down. The key for Danelle is balance. She says, 'The sweetness and acidity must be in balance, so it is important to look at this when making and blending the wine.' This balance is what pulls the Four Cousins range into line and changes what could have been a sickly sweet gloop-fest into a refreshing, attractive drink. 'Don't think too hard about it – feel free to chill it down with a block or two of ice on a hot day and enjoy.'

Real men do drink pink drinks and real men definitely

drink rosé wine.

4

SWEET AND SEMI-SWEET ROSÉS (PINK WINES)

IF PEOPLE WANT TO BE FAIRLY SURE THAT THE WINE THEY'RE GOING TO DRINK IS SWEET, THEN CHANCES ARE THEY'LL PLUMP FOR A PINK.

There must be more misconceptions surrounding rosé wines than almost any other category of wine and we'll come to those in a second. But, first, what makes a wine rosé in the first place and why is there such a wide variety of pink colours available?

Here's a quick multiple-choice quiz for you:
Pink wine is pink because:

a - The winemaker is a woman.
b - Someone made a mistake and mixed two lots of wine together.
c - Cochineal beetles love grapes and get mixed up in the crushers, adding the colour.

Actually, it's none of those. I was just messing with you. All the colour in wine comes from the skins of the grapes. All grape juice is white, so red grape juice starts out in life as white grape juice, then, gradually, the colour is leached from the skins to turn the liquid red. En route to becoming a red wine, it goes through ever-deepening shades of pink the longer the juice remains in contact with the skins, so if a winemaker is making a rosé wine, then as soon as he is happy with the colour, all he has to do is remove the skins and, hey presto, pink wine.

In Europe, pink wine can be made only from black grapes (with the exception of champagne), but in South Africa, you could actually have got away with answering 'b' in the quiz above because sometimes that is exactly what winemakers do – mix some red wine into a larger volume of white wine to make it pink. It doesn't happen all that often for the most part, although it's not uncommon to hear of wines being 'colour adjusted' before bottling.

BLANC DE NOIR

This is a term that you'll often see on rosé wine labels. Translated from French, it means 'white from black'. In reality, this mostly means a very pale rosé. There is hardly any contact with the grapeskins, so it is virtually a white wine made from black grapes. Nowadays, most wineries use the name of the black grape variety instead (e.g. Merlot rosé, Pinotage rosé), particularly if their wine is dry because blanc de noir wines have a bit of a reputation for being on the sweeter side of life.

MYTHS AND MISCONCEPTIONS ABOUT ROSÉ WINES

Right, let's slay a few of these shall we?

MYTH 1   All rosé is sweet

This is just twisted logic because colour and sweetness have absolutely zero in common – it's just that, in the past, MOST rosé had a healthy dose of sugar to help it go down. The trend nowadays is towards drier styles, particularly from the posher producers. How can you tell if it's dry? Well, if you're lucky, they'll tell you on the label, but otherwise, here is my VERY rough rule of thumb – if it's in a clear bottle with a white label and a silver screwcap, chances are it's dry!

MYTH 2   Pink wine is for girls

Actually, I don't even know why I'm wasting my time answering this myth. Unlike the irritating sexism of a 'ladies steak' (quite apart from the awful punctuation), there is no such thing as a 'ladies' wine'. Real men do drink pink drinks and real men definitely drink rosé wine – it's as simple as that. But if you still need convincing, ask yourself this – if Brad Pitt* can make a pink wine, then how much more macho do you want it to be? I rest my case.

MYTH 3   Pink wine is only for an aperitif

If you suggest this to a Frenchman or a Spaniard, they would laugh like drains. All around the Mediterranean, the drink of choice is rosé and particularly with food. All the flavours of the Med – garlic, herbs, olives, lush salads, fresh

---

* Brad Pitt and Angelina Jolie's estate, Château Miraval, in France, produced 2012's best rosé!

seafood – are perfect with pink wine, so don't just sip it beforehand, give it a go with your meal as well and see what I mean.

Here's a couple of pinks to try if you like them a touch on the sweeter side. They're fresh and crisp, and both are wicked with food.

TRY THESE

KNORHOEK TWO CUBS ROSÉ

Cheery quaffer with sweet red berries and cherries, ending in a clean, fresh finish. Perfect with spicy Chinese food.

LANZERAC ALMA MATER ROSÉ

This has been newly relaunched, still in the now-famous teardrop-shaped Lanzerac bottle, and is sweet but not sticky, fresh but not bitter. A great food wine.

AND WITH
FOOD

As with the sweet and off-dry whites, matching your pink wine with spicy food is an excellent idea. You can try a wasabi-rubbed tuna steak, or a cumin-spiced Moroccan chicken salad, and both will go well with the sweet fruitiness of the wine. Or you could go the other direction and look for umami-laden foods and see how they fare. Umami (oo-mar-mee) is the Japanese word for the fifth taste and is usually best described as an intense savouriness. Foods high in umami include Marmite, anchovies, soy sauce and nori (dried seaweed). These foods can cause problems when matched with acidic whites or tannic reds, but a touch of sweetness and the ripe fruit-packed flavours of an off-dry rosé can match them very well indeed. Try it with sushi and my new fave match for pink wines – anything involving tangy, metallic, lip-smacking blue cheese. Softens, rounds and smoothes it out in an instant.

A little of what you fancy does you good

says Pete Goffe-Wood

It is a fact not universally acknowledged that most chefs make extremely good wine tasters. Because they are so used to an enormous range of foods and cooking methods, they are generally spot-on accurate when it comes to identifying flavours and aromas, even if their suggestions and associations can be slightly obscure to most of us. However, identifying the flavours doesn't necessarily make for the ability to match them with food. For that, you need to be a little bit specialised, and more than a little bit into your wines. Along with great food and wine pairers Harald Bresselschmidt of Cape Town's Aubergine and Franck Dangereux from The Foodbarn, Noordhoek, I reckon one of South Africa's finest is kitchen cowboy, *MasterChef* judge and all-round foodie God, Pete Goffe-Wood.

Pete and I go back quite a way. When I opened my restaurant in Green Point, Pete was a consultant and I think he still laughs at me because when he advised me to buy a salamander (a heating cabinet to warm up food), I thought he meant a lizard. It has been a pleasure to follow his career to the dizzy heights he is at today. Fame and fortune are all well and good, but Pete is a hands-on guy and is never happier than messing around in a kitchen, experimenting and trying something new. For Pete, the most important component in food and wine matching is the way the food feels in the mouth. 'I think we should rather be concerned with the weight of the food and the wine than the particular colour combinations. A slightly cooled Pinotage is a brilliant accompaniment for sushi, for example.'

He goes on to say that it is easy to get carried away with the whole food-matching thing and people should really just chill out. His wife, Elize, can't drink red wine, 'so we will often stick to white throughout a meal without any disastrous consequences'.

But if you are going to have a go, how do you begin to make that perfect match of food and wine? Left to his own devices, Pete generally starts with the wine and he has definite preferences for the types of wines that he thinks work best with food. 'Personally, I believe that richer, wooded whites and white blends are more universal when it comes to pairing,' he says, and these wines certainly suit his flavour-packed style of cooking. But matching food with drink is becoming increasingly sophisticated and, because Pete is a consultant to SABMiller (formerly South African Breweries), many of his food matches actually involve beer as well. 'If you like more robust and spicier foods, as I do, then beer is actually more versatile for pairing. Spirits are also good for pairing individual dishes, but make for very heavy drinking when it's an entire meal!'

I asked him what was the best food and wine matching he's ever done, the one he's most proud of. His answer: 'I'm proud of all of them, as I like to think that I put a lot of work into getting the match right. As for a favourite, I wouldn't know where to begin.'

But I do. Pete hosted and cooked for a media lunch for Nederburg that I attended. On the menu was pretty much every part of a pig except the squeak, all paired with Nederburg's Heritage Heroes series of wines. Best match? The pan-fried sweetbreads, pancetta, capers and sage with the wooded Sauvignon Blanc. Trust me, Pete, I still dream about that dish!

If you can't tell whether a wine is sweet or dry, pinch your nostrils while you taste it. This will stop your brain having the jump on you, and will make it easier to trust your taste buds.

5

KEEPING IT DRY

WHOEVER FIRST CAME UP WITH WINE-DRINKING TERMINOLOGY AND THOUGHT THAT 'DRY' WAS A GOOD WORD TO USE TO DESCRIBE A LIQUID – 'GIVE THAT MAN A BELLS'. NOT. HONESTLY, IT'S SUCH A SILLY TERM TO USE AND HIGHLY CONFUSING. HOWEVER, THAT'S THE WAY IT IS: WHEN A WINE HAS GOT VERY LOW LEVELS OF SUGAR IN IT, WE CALL IT 'DRY'.

Describing a wine as 'dry' on a label is a legal designation – it indicates that the wine must contain less than 5 g of sugar per litre of wine. Did you know that the South African wine industry is one of the most highly regulated in the world? Ain't nothing getting past the eagle-eyed folk at the Wine and Spirit Board, which is reassuring for consumers, although it can sometimes be a big headache for winemakers and marketers. This aside doesn't have a whole lot to do with this chapter but I thought I'd slip it in anyway. (On another note, did you know that the Greek national anthem has 158 verses? Amazing what you can pick up in a wine book these days, isn't it?)

Back to the matter in hand. With a dry wine, the yeast has eaten up virtually all the sugar during fermentation and has turned it all into alcohol and CO_2. No sugar (or low levels of sugar) = a dry wine, it's as simple as that. It can sometimes be difficult to work out if a wine is dry or not, particularly ones that taste of sweet fruits, such as tropical fruits, peaches and apricots. When we smell sweet things, our brains automatically tell us we're going to taste sweet things and, consequently, a lot of people get confused. If you can't tell whether a wine is sweet or dry, pinch your nostrils while you taste it. This will stop your brain having the jump on you, and will make it easier to trust your taste buds and not get carried away by your nose.

The problem with different sugar levels is that, although a wine may have been categorised as dry by the authorities, this doesn't mean that the label on the bottle will necessarily tell you this. There are some grape varieties that you can be fairly sure will be dry, but others can be a bit more confusing and none more so than South Africa's greatest white grape – Chenin Blanc.

CHENIN BLANC – SOUTH AFRICA'S GREATEST GRAPE

Poor Chenin, it seems that versatility can be its own curse. Chenin Blanc is a fabulous grape variety, definitely one of the classier and more interesting white grapes we've got in South Africa. The problem is, many people still associate it with the old sweet bulk wine known as Steen and avoid it like the plague. The reality is that while Chenin can make some of the finest sweet wines in the world, it can also make rich, ripe off-dry versions as well as crisp, fresh and zippy dry wines, and sometimes people forget this. There has been much talk in the South African wine industry in recent years about whether all Chenins should be classified in a standard way, but the jury is still out as to how this would be managed. According to Ken Forrester, the King of Chenin in South Africa, Chenin Blanc offers better value than Sauvignon Blanc at every single price point – so whether you spend R30, R50 or R150 on a bottle, you're always better off with a Chenin.

Sauvignon Blanc

This is a fairly sure bet when it comes to dryness, but even if it's not absolutely bone dry, the high levels of acidity will give the feeling of dryness anyway.

Chardonnay

Most are dry, although lower in acidity than Sauvignon. The fact that Chardonnay can get very ripe and taste of sweet fruits (such as pineapples, peaches and melons) can be confusing.

Pinot Grigio

You can expect that most of these will be dry and, again, they'll have high levels of acidity to help on the way. You'll sometimes see this wine labelled as Pinot Gris – don't worry, it's exactly the same wine: 'Grigio' is what it's called in Italy; 'Gris' is the French version of the name. Lots of grape varieties have dual European names and in South Africa, wineries just choose the one they think will help sell the most wine.

Viognier

Makes mostly dry wines but, again, like Chardonnay, they can taste of sweet fruits like apricots and peaches, so expect some aroma confusion.

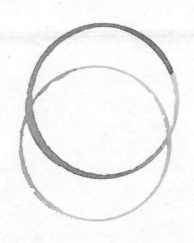

When you start dropping the sugar levels, it's always hard (hey, dieters?), so the best thing to do is not to rush it, but to take baby steps and see where you end up.

6

UNWOODED DRY WHITE AND PINK WINES

IN THE NEXT CHAPTER, WE'LL LOOK AT WHAT I MEAN WHEN I SAY 'WOODED' AND 'UNWOODED'. FOR NOW, JUST TAKE IT THAT THE WINES YOU'VE BEEN DRINKING SO FAR HAVEN'T BEEN AGED IN WOOD BARRELS AND LET'S KEEP GOING DOWN THAT TRACK.

Once you've got the hang of (and the taste for) semi-sweet and off-dry white and pink wines, the next step is to see if you can go for something a bit drier and try some wines with lower sugar levels.

DRY WINE: WHY SHOULD I?

Fair question, really. I suppose the only answer is that the vast majority of wines are dry and if you stick to sweeter wines, your choices are always going to be somewhat restricted. Look at it this way – when we were kids, we all had fairly limited food repertoires that contained simple dishes like fish fingers, Vienna sausages and mac 'n cheese served to us repeatedly. Now that we're all growed-up and adventurous, we actually enjoy a lot of the things we turned our noses up at as kids. Just think of coffee, curry and sushi. Wine is just the same – we start with the easy stuff and gradually stretch our taste boundaries until we can encompass just about anything. The secret is not to stretch too much at any one time.

IS ACID YOUR ENEMY?

It's not just the lack of sweetness that bothers people about dry wines, it's also the fact that the acidity is accentuated when there's no sugar for it to hide behind, which can make it very obtrusive and off-putting. Acidity is very important in wines and a wine without acid is flabby and boring. On the other hand, acidity is not the easiest thing in the world to enjoy – if you don't believe me, then go suck a lemon. When you drink sweeter wines, the sugar masks the acid and makes the wine more acceptable to sensitive palates, but as soon as you lose the sugar, then people start using words like 'sour', 'bitter' and 'just too dry for me' as the acid makes its presence felt.

HOW CAN YOU TELL IF A WINE HAS HIGH ACIDITY?

When you taste a wine that has high acidity, you can generally feel it immediately – a tingling sensation starts in your ears and rushes down your jawline. If you think that just sounds plain nuts (and I wouldn't blame you), then check the acidity by doing the 'drip test'. This looks quite revolting, so you might want to try it in the privacy of your own home – and definitely not in a restaurant. Take a mouthful of wine and roll it round in your mouth, then spit it out into a spittoon, cup or sink. After you've spat it out, remain leaning over the spittoon/cup/sink with your mouth open and see how long it takes before the saliva comes rushing back into your mouth and you have to close it hastily or drip from your open mouth – a most unsavoury sight for any companions! If you 'drip' within a couple of seconds, it is a high-acidity wine. If you wait for around three to five seconds, it is medium acidity and if you wait forever, then it is a wine with low acidity. Try this at home to get the feel of it and then, once you are sure you can identify acid, you won't need to do the drip test – you'll be able to recognise it while it's in your mouth.

When you start dropping the sugar levels, it's always hard (hey, dieters?), so the best thing to do is not to rush it, but to take baby steps and see where you end up. If you're a sweet-wine drinker, go back to Chapters 3 and 4, and try some of the off-dry wine recommendations included there, but if you're ready to try something a bit drier than you'd normally drink, then your best bets are unwooded Chardonnays and Chenins, and simple white blends. Scrutinise the back labels and look for wines that describe themselves as 'fruity', 'juicy' and 'soft'. Once you feel comfortable with a little bit of a sappy backbone and only when you're happy, move on and try a Sauvignon Blanc. Don't jump straight to Sauvignon Blanc just because everyone else seems to think it's God's gift to white wine. An ill-judged Sauvvie can actually take the skin off your teeth and put you off dry wines for life.

The first three wines I recommend below are blends. Don't fall into the trap of thinking a blend is a winemaker's way of hiding all the crap he can't sell as single varieties. A good blend should be greater than the sum of its parts, with each variety helping the other out and filling each other's gaps.

BON COURAGE HILLSIDE WHITE

Fresh, sappy blend of Colombard and Chardonnay with lots of sweet citrus fruit and a clean finish.

GROOTE POST THE OLD MAN'S BLEND

One of my favourite blends – Sauvignon and Chenin Blancs with a little bit of Semillon. An easy-drinking wine packed with fruit – total crowd-pleaser.

FLAGSTONE NOON GUN

This used to contain seven different varieties, but they've slimmed it down somewhat and now it's a peachy, fresh, happy drink and a great wine for beginners.

Moving on now to Chenins, unwooded Chardonnays and, finally, Sauvignon Blancs. Try this lot for starters:

SIMONSIG CHENIN BLANC

Every bottle I buy seems to leak. I mean, that has to be the reason that I pour myself one glass and when I look up again, the rest of the bottle has disappeared. Doesn't it?

KEN FORRESTER PETIT CHENIN

Start small or 'Petit' and work your way up, because there's no better starting place than this wine. Soft yellow fruits, cheery acidity, totally non-scary in any way whatsoever.

EIKENDAL JANINA UNWOODED CHARDONNAY

Eikendal are Chardonnay experts and this is their entry level to deliciousness. Lots of ripe tropical fruit, crisp acidity, fresh finish.

SAUVIGNON.COM SAUVIGNON BLANC

This comes from Sauvvie supremo Thys Louw, at Diemersdal, and is made in a fruity, fresh, easy-drinking style that is perfect for people new to the variety.

WELMOED SAUVIGNON BLANC

This is a good-value range of wines, readily available, correct and well made. Clean, crisp and packed with ripe fruit – a good intro to Sauvignon Blanc.

And for pink-wine lovers, try these two. Both have lively acidity and are very close to being dry:

ALLÉE BLEUE STARLETTE SHIRAZ ROSÉ

Lots and lots of cherries and berries mixed up with just a hint of sweetness, and a dryish finish.

DELHEIM PINOTAGE ROSÉ

Packed with fruit and technically just off-dry, this is a real crowd-pleaser, which will keep every pink-lover perky and pert all evening.

AND WITH FOOD

As for matching dry wines with food, if the acidity is proving a bit tricky, then tone it down by matching it with a food that is also high in acidity. Fish or shellfish laced with loads of lemon will make the wine seem a bit sweeter, while the acidity in the wine will help cut through richer fish dishes such as smoked salmon. But these are very versatile wines, so my advice would be not to stress too much about finding perfect matches – just enjoy drinking them!

Sort out your wine list

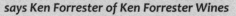

says Ken Forrester of Ken Forrester Wines

An enthusiast is appealing, but a fanatic is irresistible. And Ken Forrester is fanatical about his Chenins – all of them, from the dry Petit Chenin, the delicately wooded Reserve, the bubbly Sparklehorse, through to his rich and sublime FMC (technically, this stands for Forrester Meinert Chenin, but in the cellar, you'll more often find it referred to by its very apt name of F***ing Marvellous Chenin!) and finishing up with the luscious 'T' Noble Late Harvest.

Chenin was Ken's first love. He started his drinking career with these wines produced in the Loire Valley, in France. When he realised that South Africa has more Chenin than France and, in many cases, it is better quality in South Africa (there are pockets of century-old bushvines around the country), and that South Africa has lots of the essential 'cool sunshine' needed to ripen the grape to perfection, he decided to become a Chenin specialist.

The fact that you've actually heard of Chenin Blanc at all is largely due to the efforts of Ken, Bruwer Raats, Irina von Holdt and a few other growers who started bucking the trend for Sauvignon and Chardonnay around twenty years ago. And 'trendiness' is an important term in the case of Chenin because, right now, sadly, trendy it ain't. Ken feels this is on the cusp of changing, but if we are ever going to see Chenin take its rightful place at the top of the drinks chain, we need to do something about how it is marketed, particularly in restaurants.

How many restaurant wine lists have you seen that have eight Sauvignon Blancs and only one Chenin? I used to own a restaurant and many people told me not to bother listing Chenins because nobody wanted to drink them, thus creating a self fulfilling prophecy for all who believed such rubbish. You may not realise it, but many restaurants charge a listing fee to wineries if they want their wines to be included in a wine list and, equally so, some larger wine operations will shower a restaurant with gifts in the form of free umbrellas, menu covers, ice buckets and the like in exchange for having the majority of wines from their stable on the list. If you think wine lists look the same from one restaurant to the next, or if you are seeing the same wines on quite a lot of lists, then one of these two things may be in play. Although not illegal and not always necessarily involving bad wines, these practices do make it hard for smaller wineries or more unusual wines to get a look in at the bigger restaurants. And of course, it's pretty dispiriting to see the same-old, same-old wines cropping up time and time again.

This is what Ken wants to see changed, particularly in favour of Chenin Blanc. 'Too many wine lists are badly constructed and unbalanced,' he says. Instead, we must 'educate the public, get the public to complain when confronted with poor choice and lousy wine lists. Keep on making ever-improving wines from Chenin, keep marketing quality Chenin and, soon enough, people will realise the charms and virtues of this wonderful grape.'

He feels it's particularly important that restaurants improve their Chenin choices because there is no better wine to go with food. With his restaurateur hat on (Ken co-owns the 96 Winery Road restaurant in Stellenbosch), he extols the virtues of eating food and drinking Chenin at the same time. Recommendations range from 'a bowl of creamy mussels with a simple, fresh, unwooded wine, to a full, rich dish like a grilled crayfish or lobster drizzled with citrus butter, or seared scallops with a bacon and light truffle dressing, jumbo prawns on the braai with lemon dipping sauce, mild Malay-style curries or a spicy seafood paella – all served with full-bodied, barrel-aged Chenins.'

For Ken, Chenin Blanc is the Madonna of the wine world – 'beautiful, poised, feminine and confident, but all the while supremely capable of being totally wild, almost out of control and epically, incredibly alluring.'

And who wouldn't want to drink something with a description like that?

Wine can taste of yellow fruit, red fruit, black fruit, green fruit, cooked fruit, fresh fruit, mixed fruit, confected fruit. It can also taste of veggies – peas, beans, peppers. And herbs. And spices. Pretty much any flavour or aroma you can think of, I bet you could find it in a wine if you searched hard enough.

7

Wine tech   NO. 3

WHAT'S THE DEAL WITH WOOD?

ONE OF THE MOST AMAZING THINGS ABOUT WINE IS THAT IT TASTES OF SO MANY DIFFERENT THINGS.

Interestingly enough, it rarely tastes of grapes, because the grapes we eat are completely different varieties from those used to make most wines. (If you *want* to try wines that do taste of grapes, go for a Muscat, or Moscato, wine.) Wine can taste of yellow fruit, red fruit, black fruit, green fruit, cooked fruit, fresh fruit, mixed fruit, confected fruit. It can also taste of veggies –

peas, beans, peppers. And herbs. And spices. And strange things like leather, tobacco, sweat (bet you're dying to put this wine in your mouth now, aren't you) and even petrol – I kid you not. Pretty much any flavour or aroma you can think of, I bet you could find it in a wine if you searched hard enough.

So where do all these flavours come from? Is someone standing over a tank of wine and tipping in 5 kg of lemons and 3 kg of green peppers? No – that's illegal, and if you get caught you're in big trouble. What's actually going on is that each different variety of grape has different flavour compounds within it, and these are identical to those that give the lemon flavour to lemons, the pepper flavour to peppers, and so on. When our noses and taste buds identify those chemical compounds, our brains associate them with ones that are already familiar to us and so we think we're tasting lemons and peppers, whereas, in fact, it's just the same little combination of chemicals. Apparently, humans can identify between 4 000 and 10 000 odour molecules, and if you think you're no good at identifying them, the good news is that you can improve with practice. Good excuse to drink more wine, huh!

SO, NO FLAVOURS ADDED AT ALL THEN?

As I said earlier, the laws governing winemaking are really very strict and you may not add any additional flavourings to your wine – with the single exception of oak. The use of oak in winemaking is a happy coincidence. Centuries before glass bottles were invented, the best vessels for making and keeping wine in were wooden ones. People discovered they liked the extra flavours the oak added, so continued to use it long after other containers and materials for producing and storing wine had been invented. But why oak and not any other wood? Others have been tried, and various types of wood – such as acacia, mahogany, cherry and more – are still used in the industry today, but everyone keeps returning to oak because, to be frank, it just tastes better. And that's the real reason, nothing fancier than that.

WHAT EFFECT DOES OAK HAVE ON WINE?

Oak does a couple of things to wine, but much of its effect depends on the age of the oak used. The first use is to add flavour. If a winemaker uses brand-new oak barrels, they will add a lot of toasty, buttery, spicy flavours to the wine. After the wine has been in them for a few months, or perhaps a year or so, the winemaker takes it out, bottles it, cleans the barrel and puts in the next batch of wine the following year. This barrel then becomes known as 'a second-fill' barrel because it is being used for the second time. The oak flavour it imparts is now not as strong as the previous year, but the barrel still adds toasty/spicy notes to the wine. And, then, the following year, the wine is removed, the barrel cleaned, new wine put in and now the barrel becomes 'a third-fill'. Etcetera, etcetera. Most winemakers use barrels about four times before they sell them to be cut in half and have flowers planted in them.

COMING UP FOR OXYGEN

The second use for oak barrels is to help 'soften' and mature the wine, especially reds. Small amounts of oxygen are able to access the wine inside and start to interact with the flavours and tannins in red wines, causing the wine to become smoother and easier to drink – see Chapter 13 for more. You have to carefully control how much oxygen is allowed to be in contact with the wine because there is the risk it might oxidise. What's that, I hear you ask? Let me give you an example. If you cut an apple in half and leave the halves cut-side up on the plate, they go brown, don't they? What's happening is that the oxygen in the air reacts with the fruit and starts the process of rotting it. This is called 'oxidation' and the same thing happens to wine if it's left exposed to the air for too long – after all, it's just another fruit, really. Winemakers take care not to let this happen by restricting the amount of oxygen allowed in contact with the wine either by filling the barrels as full as they can or by adding sulphur dioxide (SO_2) to keep the oxygen at bay.

As I said, oak is the only flavour allowed in wine, but you can add that flavour in various ways, and the way you choose is generally dependent on how much money you've got to spend. A new barrel from Europe or America costs around R10 000 (you know, they always say that the way to make a small fortune in the wine industry is to start with a big one), so, for many people, a couple of new barrels a year is all they can afford.

If you can't manage to buy all the barrels you need, then you can get oak flavour in your wine by using staves – these are planks of oak that hang in a tank of wine. These used to be frowned upon by wine snobs, but it is a cost-effective way of getting the oak flavour into the wine and with the addition of some new winemaking know-how, it works very well. If you're into chocolate/coffee Pinotages, then this is the method generally used to produce those flavours in your fave wines.

Next on the cost scale is a giant teabag of woodchips, which is dangled into the wine so it can soak up the oak flavour. The cheapest option is to add oak essence, which gives tannin and a little flavour. If you can add oak essence and it's so much cheaper than a barrel, then why do people bother with barrels at all? The answer is all to do with how well the oak integrates into the wine. The long, slow seeping of flavour from barrels gives the best results in the long run.

FRENCH, HUNGARIAN, ROMANIAN, AMERICAN – WHY DON'T WE USE SOUTH AFRICAN OAK?

I often get asked this question – after all, it would make much more sense to use our own local oak, save money, reduce the carbon footprint, etc., etc. But, in this case, unfortunately, local isn't lekker. Most of the oak trees grown in South Africa are the wrong kind for making into barrels and the hot climate means that the trees grow much faster here than in cooler areas of the world, so the grain of the wood isn't tight enough. The long and short of it is that barrels made of South African oak will leak. Which is never a good thing if they contain wine.

WHAT DOES OAK DO TO THE FLAVOUR OF A WINE?

Finally, the all-important question. We know an oak barrel can allow oxygen in and soften and smooth wines, but what does it add to the flavour? Well, it adds a whole extra dimension to a wine, and oak from different parts of the world adds different, characteristic notes. Most barrels are charred or singed inside before they're used. This is called 'toasting', and the level of toasting will also affect the final taste.

In the main, a wooded wine will have some or all of the following flavours:

- Toast
- Butter
- Smoke
- Vanilla (especially if the barrel is made from American oak)
- Toffee or caramel
- Spice – especially sweet spices like nutmeg, clove and cinnamon
- Coffee
- Tobacco
- Coconut (especially if the barrel is made from American oak)

Virtually all red wines are wooded, so the descriptors above are commonly used when referring to reds, but not all white and pink wines have been wooded, so if you see words like those in the list on the back label, then it's a good clue that the wine has had contact with some sort of oak. People also use terms such as 'barrel-fermented', 'barrel-aged' or 'oak-aged' to indicate there's wood in there somewhere. If you prefer unwooded wines, then look for words such as 'crisp, fresh, refreshing, zesty, clean, tangy and citrusy' instead. And, if you're lucky, the winemaker will tell you on the label that the wine is 'unoaked' or 'unwooded'. But don't count on it.

To my mind, oak should be like your parents – there, in the background, keeping an eye on you, making sure you don't get into trouble, but still letting you have your own personality and flair. The fruit flavours should always be the star. But having a little extra dimension, another layer of complexity and interest, is what makes great wines great.

8

WOODED WHITE WINES

THIS CHAPTER IS, IN MY HUMBLE OPINION, ONE OF THE BIGGEST STEPS YOU CAN MAKE EN ROUTE TO BECOMING A WELL-ROUNDED WINE DRINKER.

In fact, it's fair to say that for many people, this is a step too far and they see no need whatsoever to take it, preferring to stick with unwooded wines for the duration of their natural lives. Why are these wines so problematic?

Here are a couple of reasons:

1. They cost more, so expectations are higher. Wooded wines nearly always cost more than their equivalent unwooded counterparts, simply because, as I mentioned in the previous chapter, a barrel costs around R10 000 and that money must get accounted for somewhere. Of course, not all wineries use brand-new barrels, but all wood – whether it's staves, chips or essence – has a price. When you pay more for a bottle, you expect to get more and, sadly, this isn't always the case.

2. Where's the fruit? Modern winemaking has really concentrated on delivering big, fat, smacks-in-the-face of fruit – easily identifiable and understood flavours of citrus, tropical fruit, peaches and strawberries. Wood, however, adds another dimension to the mix and changes the nature of that fresh, clean fruit. If it's done well, you find yourself thinking of loads of different types of cooked fruit, from stewed, baked and caramelised, to marmalade and jam. But if it's done badly, you don't even taste the fruit at all, as it's all hidden behind a mass of chewy, mouth-drying, splintery wood.

There is no doubt that some people in the wine industry have done wood a big disservice over the years. Personally (and with no agenda that in any way involves the cricket), I blame the Australians. Drinking wine in the 1990s – the heyday of Australian wine – you got the impression that every bottle was there purely to showcase the woodchips because it was just one long succession of chewy, toasty, charry bottles after another and this certainly put me off oak for a helluva long time. It's back to our old friend that we discussed in Chapter 3 – we need to have some balance. And in no other category is balance as important as in wooded white and pink wines.

(I have to admit that the Aussies have mightily improved when it comes to the use of oak. And their cricket is getting better as well. Damn it.)

BALANCE IS EVERYTHING

To my mind, oak should be like your parents – there, in the background, keeping an eye on you, making sure you don't get into trouble, but still letting you have your own personality and flair. No one wants to drink wood juice – if we did, we'd have found a way to pulverise planks by now and would be guzzling those by the bottle instead – so the fruit flavours should always be the star. But having a little extra dimension, another layer of complexity and interest, is what makes great wines great. And good oaking can do that by subtly enhancing the fruit, and making the wine change and evolve both in the bottle and in your mouth.

This isn't actually something you see mentioned on wine labels, probably because it sounds a bit too technical. But it is something that happens to lots of wines, particularly those that spend time in contact with oak, so it's a good thing to know about. Basically, it isn't a fermentation as such, but more of a bacterial conversion, though I guess that doesn't sound as sexy. With malolactic fermentation, a specific bacteria, either present naturally or one that can be introduced into the wine, changes the nature of the acids. In the process, the green, crisp, appley malic acids are converted into much softer, creamier, yoghurty lactic acids. This has the effect of making the wine softer, smoother, richer and more rounded. Most wines that undergo 'malo' (as it's commonly referred to) are wooded wines because allowing malo enhances the effect of the wood.

A lot of people like malo, particularly with wooded Chardonnays and Chenins, because it makes them more satisfying wines to drink. Equally so, a lot of people hate it and prefer fresher, lighter, more zippy wines, so some winemakers try their best to stop this conversion taking place by lowering temperatures in the cellar and adding certain chemicals to kill the bacteria. To my mind, the best option is to make a few different batches of wine, some with malo and some without, and then blend them before bottling. The blending makes for some richness plus some freshness and, overall, a much more balanced wine.

If you're going to try wooded wines for the first time, I would recommend that you find something that is lightly wooded. The first few here are good examples – they have some creaminess, but are still fresh and enticing.

MULDERBOSCH STEEN OP HOUT CHENIN BLANC

A proportion of this wine has spent some time in barrels but the rest is made in a stainless-steel tank. This is a great starter wine for wood-newbies: fresh, appetising, yellow-apple and citrus flavours, with just a hint of vanilla.

KWV CLASSIC COLLECTION CHARDONNAY

Zippy and fresh with just a hint of cream, this is a nice transition from unwooded to wooded, offering plenty of soft, ripe, yellow fruit.

THE WOLFTRAP WHITE

Many people's first choice as a bargain white wine, this is a blend of Viognier, Chenin Blanc and Grenache Blanc, all edged with a little spicy oak. Nicely done.

Once you're happy with a little hint of wood, trade up to something a bit more structured. Try these – they have more oak influence but are still well-balanced wines:

FAIRVIEW NUROK WHITE

A blend of various grapes but mainly Viognier, this has been sensitively oaked and balances the creamy, waxy notes with a freshening acidity throughout.

EIKENDAL RESERVE CHARDONNAY

The epitome of balance with the ripe green and yellow fruit nestling happily alongside fresh acidity, gentle oak and a zippy minerality. Rich and creamy when you need it to be, lively and elegant when that is required – wonderful drinking always.

CREDO CHENIN BLANC

This comes from nicely mature vines, which tend to produce fewer, but more concentrated grapes so the wine can handle the barrel fermentation and subsequent ageing in oak that it receives. Lashings of flavour, intensity and balance – a fabulous food wine.

AND WITH
FOOD

Wow, where should I start? These big, bold and robust wines will stand up to all kinds of food – including a steak, if that's what you want them to accompany. Be careful about matching wooded wines with delicate fish dishes though, such as grilled sole or plain oysters, because they may overwhelm the fish, but you're pretty safe with chicken, fish, pork, cheese – you name it. Go forth and experiment!

'ABC' re-explained

by Nico Grobler of Eikendal Vineyards

After the Australians had invaded the UK with all their woody, toasty, tooth-picking Chardonnays, there came (unsurprisingly) a backlash against Chardonnay. The only problem was that a lot of people didn't realise that what they didn't like was the oak and instead blamed the grape variety, so 'anything but Chardonnay', or 'ABC', became a phrase regularly heard at wine tastings and in wine bars. I know for a fact that the problem was the wood, and not the grape variety, because lots of people would approach me at tasting events and say, 'ABC, darling!', whereupon I would give them a Chablis (which is an unwooded Chardonnay), and they would discover that they loved it.

I'm not the only one who did – and still does – that. Nico Grobler, winemaker at Eikendal Vineyards and self-confessed Chardonnay-nut, says he does it all the time with his unwooded Chardonnay, the Janina. 'The great thing about Janina is that it has all the fundamentals of good Chardonnay, but without the influence of oak,' he says. 'So people get an idea of what the Chardonnay actually tastes like without being scared off by any oaky flavours. It is a great tool and our strongest-growing brand.'

Because Chardonnay is such a willing and accommodating grape, Nico says it can often fall victim to the 'three too muches' – too much alcohol, too much oak and too much fruit. 'The fundamentals of great Chardonnay are freshness, tightness and minerality,' he says. 'Great Chardonnay is built up by a lot of small complexities, creating a big, complex wine overall.' He believes that we are making much better Chardonnays in South Africa than previously, especially in the last five years. 'Winemakers are much better travelled and have much more experience of other styles,' he believes, 'so there is no place for too much butteriness, oak and alcohol.'

Nico's influences are all Old World (which, in the case of Chardonnay, means Burgundy in France) and his winemaking mentor is a chap called Bruno Lorenzon from French wine region Mercurey. Under Lorenzon's guidance, he has replanted the vineyards and changed the way he works with oak in the winery, allowing the flavoursome dead yeast cells (or lees – see Chapter 15) to be reused from one year to the next. All these various factors aim to increase those complex and interesting notes, while the influence of the oak decreases the longer the barrel is used. 'When you explain what you are doing with Chardonnay to people and then they taste my wine, they always love it,' he claims. 'In my mind, there is no more room for "anything but Chardonnay" people. I think we should still call ourselves ABC-ers but demand "another beautiful Chardonnay" instead!'

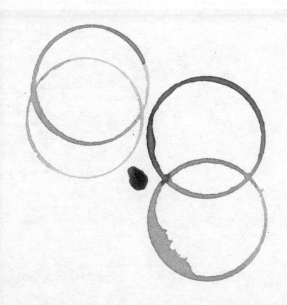

Generally, Chenin offers very good value for money at all price levels. It comes in a range of styles too, from bone dry to semi-sweet to luscious dessert wines, and it's sometimes oaked, particularly the more serious examples.

9

WHITE GRAPES 101

BEFORE WE GO CHARGING OFF INTO THE WORLD OF RED WINES, I'M GOING TO TAKE A MOMENT TO GIVE YOU SOME INFO ON SOME OF THE MOST POPULAR WHITE GRAPE VARIETIES YOU'LL FIND IN SOUTH AFRICA. HERE WE GO.

CHENIN BLANC ('SHUN-AN BLONK' – THE FRENCH PRONUNCIATION, BUT IN SOUTH AFRICA WE TEND TO SAY 'SHEN-IN BLONK')

This is South Africa's most-planted grape variety and certainly our most interesting. Generally, Chenin offers very good value for money at all price levels, ranging from sub-R30 bottles to over R300. It comes in a range of styles too, from bone-dry to semi-sweet to luscious dessert wines, and it's sometimes oaked, particularly the more serious examples. Flavours – yellow and green apples and pears, some citrus notes, melons, pineapples, stone fruit.

SAUVIGNON BLANC ('SEW-VIN-YON BLONK')

South Africa's most popular white grape, this is generally planted in cooler climates in order to keep the freshening acidity. It's nearly always a dry wine and is rarely wooded, which makes it popular with oak haters. Flavours – green apples, asparagus, cat's pee (☺), green peppers, grass, green and yellow citrus in really cool regions, through to guavas, granadillas and other tropical fruits in slightly hotter parts of the country.

CHARDONNAY ('SHAR-DUNN-AY')

The world's best-travelled white grape and one that has a great track record in South Africa, to the extent that some punters even suggest that it should be our flagship white variety instead of Chenin. It makes a range of wines from light and delicately fruity to big, powerful, oaky monsters that can last for a decade with ease. It also makes, or contributes to, some of the best sparkling wines in the country (more on these in Chapter 16). Flavours – all colours of citrus, peaches, melons, pineapples, mangoes, tropical fruit.

COLOMBAR/COLOMBARD ('COL-OM-BAR')

Two spellings, same grape. This is mostly used to produce brandy but is also a big component in inexpensive dry and off-dry whites. Flavours – fairly neutral (it makes the kinds of wines that my husband says 'just taste and smell of wine and that's it'!) with hints of citrus, apples and some honeyed notes.

VIOGNIER ('VEE-ON-NEE-AY')

Think 'lasagne' when you pronounce the 'gn' in Viognier and you'll get it right! This is a grape variety growing in popularity in South Africa because it does well in warmer climates and therefore makes quite alcoholic wines. Most winemakers oak them, although far more gently than in the past, which is a good thing. Flavours – distinctive notes of stone fruit (apricots and peaches) with flowers and spice.

RIESLING ('REESS-LING')

It is important to know that we have two kinds of Riesling in South Africa. The 'proper' stuff, which originally comes from Germany, and used to be labelled as Rhine Riesling or Weisser Riesling, and the less good stuff, which is now labelled Cape Riesling or Paarl Riesling. In the past, a confusion came about as to which variety was planted and a grape called Crouchen Blanc ('crew-shon-blonk') was mistaken for Riesling and it is this which now makes Cape/Paarl Riesling. Proper Riesling is one of the finest grapes in the world, making a range of styles from bone dry to some of the most expensive dessert wines. Flavours – flowers, honey, orange and yellow citrus, apples and when it ages, expect to smell some petrol or kerosene.

PINOT GRIGIO/PINOT GRIS ('PEE-NO GREE-JEO'/'PEE-NO GREE')

These are very popular wines in the UK and the variety is on the up in South Africa as well. People can label it any way they like, but it's the same grape ('Grigio' is simply the Italian spelling and 'Gris' is the French). It generally has the high acidity you'd expect from Italian grape varieties and is usually unwooded – another reason for its popularity. Flavours – apples, pears, some lemons and melons, a little nuttiness with age.

SEMILLON ('SEM-EE-YON')

Not a particularly well-known grape variety in South Africa these days, although it used to be extremely popular. Semillon is mostly used in top-quality white blends either with its partner from France – Sauvignon Blanc – or, increasingly, with any combination of Chenin, Chardonnay, Viognier and more. Likes oak. Flavours – lemons, limes, flowers and, with age, honey, waxiness, incense and wet wool.

Finally, here are a few other grape varieties that are also used in South African wine:

RHÔNE GRAPES – ROUSSANNE, GRENACHE BLANC

These originate from the Rhône Valley, in southern France, and, along with Viognier, are becoming popular because they can handle heat (and some of South Africa's wine regions are hot-climate). Mostly, these varieties are used in blends but keep an eye out for producers such as KWV, The Foundry and Rustenberg, which are starting to make them as standalone wines, and expect another Rhône variety – Marsanne – to make an appearance very soon. Flavours, broadly speaking, are similar to those of Viognier but with less overt stone fruit and a little more nuts, flowers and hay.

AROMATIC GRAPES
– GEWÜRZTRAMINER, BUKETTRAUBE, HANEPOOT/MUSCAT

The first two are produced in quite small volumes and generally make off-dry wines with spicy flavours of litchis and rose petals. Hanepoot is the South African name for one of the Muscat varieties and usually makes sweet wines, either as a single variety or in inexpensive blends. South Africa has a lot of Muscat grapes, which can be made into fortified dessert wines but, increasingly, Muscat is being used in low-alcohol, slightly fizzy numbers, perfect for beginner wine drinkers and very popular overseas.

What do the grapeskins impart? Wonderful, vibrant, rich colour; stout tannins to make the wine have a bit of oomph and bite; and, most importantly, lots of yummy, juicy flavour as well. Here's how to turn your pale juice into a roaring red.

10

RED WINES (THE EXTRA STEP OF GETTING COLOUR)

AT THIS STAGE, I'D LIKE TO REMIND YOU THAT ALL THE WINES WE'VE TALKED ABOUT SO FAR COULD ACTUALLY HAVE BEEN MADE FROM BLACK GRAPES – ALL YOU HAVE TO DO IS MAKE SURE THE JUICE DOES NOT COME INTO CONTACT WITH THE SKINS.

However, so much goodness is contained in the skins of black grapes that it's not surprising people want to use them in their wines. What do the grapeskins impart? Wonderful, vibrant, rich colour; stout tannins to make the wine have a bit of oomph and bite; and, most importantly, lots of yummy, juicy flavour as well. Here's how to turn your pale juice into a roaring red.

SUCKING THE MARROW OUT OF LIFE

The key to making red wine lies in extracting the colour from the skins. When you make white wine, generally speaking you squash the grapes and then squeeze the juice out, throwing the skins away after they've been pressed dry. You then add yeast, which starts the fermentation. (If this sounds new to you, back you go to read through Wine tech 1 to remind yourself of the process. Go on. You've clearly been drinking too much.)

In the case of making red wine, you squash the grapes, but before you squeeze everything out of them, you start the fermentation by adding the yeast directly into the big, fat, soggy, stodgy mess that is the crushed grapes. Fermentation looks quite aggressive and the carbon dioxide makes the wine bubble and froth as if it were boiling. The gas rises to the top of the tank and as it makes its way up through the wine, it carries the grapeskins with it, and before long, there will be a thick crust of skins forming at the top of the wine.

This crust of skins, or 'cap', as they call it, gets very thick – so thick that you can actually stand on it without it breaking. But, even though this is quite a cool trick, the floating cap doesn't really do the wine much good. You see, in order for the wine to absorb all the colour, it needs to be in contact with the skins, and when the skins form this cap, only the thin layer of wine immediately underneath the cap actually gets the benefit. If you don't break the cap and mix the skins up with the wine, the result will be a very pale pink drink indeed.

Winemakers break up the cap in two ways. They either stand on top of the tank and do it manually with a big stick or a golf club, or whatever, and push the skins down to the bottom, or they attach a pipe to the bottom of the tank and pump the pale juice in a circular motion back to the top of the tank. This acts like a high-pressure hose and breaks up the cap into individual grapeskins, which become mixed up with the wine once more.

AGAIN AND AGAIN ...

Of course, once you've done this once, the carbon dioxide kicks into action again and lifts the grapeskins back up to form another cap, so you have to repeat this pumping over/punching down at regular intervals until the fermentation has come to an end and you have all the colour and tannin you want in the wine. If for no other reason, this is why I would never be a winemaker. Who on earth wants to head back to the cellar late on a Friday night to get your hands stained with lots of icky, gritty grapeskins when you could be sitting in a bar drinking wine instead? Thank God most winemakers don't think the same as I do, is all I can say!

WHAT IS TANNIN AND WHY IS IT NEEDED IN WINE?

We've used the word 'tannin' quite a lot, but what actually is it? Tannin occurs in other things apart from red wine. For example, if you make a cup of tea and leave the teabag in the cup for too long, you will notice a scummy skin of tannin forming on the sides of the cup. If I say that tannin is the mouth-puckering, gum-drying, make-your-mouth-go-all-dog's-bum substance that causes you to want to scrape your tongue and scratch your teeth, you may well be forgiven for asking, why the hell should I want that in my mouth? The thing is that tannin has two very important jobs to do in red wines:

- It stops the wine from being a soupy, gloopy mouthful of alcoholic jam or fruit juice and gives it structure.
- It helps the wine to keep fresh for longer and allows it time to evolve. This may not seem too important if you buy wines in the morning and drink them by dinner time, but if a wine is good enough in the first place and if it has enough of a natural preservative like tannin and if you can

bear to wait, then tannin will make sure that your wine stays in good shape, that it changes and evolves, and becomes more interesting as the months and years roll by.

The best way to show how beneficial tannin is for wine (and how yukky it tastes on its own) is to get hold of some black grapes. Carefully peel the skin off one of them and make a little pile of skin by the side of your plate – can you see how your fingers become stained with that lovely purple-red colour? Now pick up that pile of grapeskin and eat it – how shivery-down-the-back-of-your-spine is that? It's bitter and dry and nasty, but it gives you an idea of what tannins taste like. Now eat the peeled grape on its own – it's sweet and you can taste the acidity, but there's not much flavour. Finally, eat a whole, unpeeled grape and you'll see how the flavour is enhanced: the tannin is now more subtle and doesn't bother you – the sweetness is balanced by the tannins; and, overall, it's a much more pleasurable eating experience.

And that – in a grapeskin – is why you need tannins in your wine.

Nothing, but nothing, will ever be better in your mouth than an elegant, fragrant, mature Bordeaux blend, cellared in a dark place for a decade and opened reverently and peacefully with the very best of friends.

11

LIGHT AND FRUITY RED WINES

FOR SOME OF YOU, THIS MAY BE 'THE CHAPTER TOO FAR'. MOST PEOPLE START OUT ON WHITE WINES BECAUSE THEY'RE EASIER TO HANDLE AND PLENTY OF PEOPLE ARE HAPPY TO STAY WITH WHITES FOR THE REST OF THEIR DRINKING LIVES. AND THAT'S FINE – THERE IS ABSOLUTELY NO NEED FOR YOU TO DRAG YOUR TASTE BUDS THROUGH THE GRIT AND GRIP OF RED WINES. THIS ISN'T AN IRONMAN COMPETITION AND THERE ARE NO 'COOL POINTS' AWARDED FOR SUFFERING WHILE YOU DRINK. SO, IF YOU WANT TO STOP READING THIS BOOK AT THIS POINT, THAT'S OKAY BY ME. THANKS FOR COMING THIS FAR, AND I WISH YOU HAPPY DRINKING.

On the other hand, if you feel like giving red wines a go, then that's groovy too because nothing is as satisfying as a hearty glass of red wine on a cold evening. Nothing goes quite as well with red meat as red wine. And nothing, but nothing, will ever be better in your mouth than an elegant, fragrant, mature Bordeaux blend, cellared in a dark place for a decade and opened reverently and peacefully with the very best of friends. I'm sorry, I got a bit carried away there, but I think you know what I mean. If you can get into them, then red wines are the business.

COME ON DOWN, THE PRICE IS RIGHT

My father always said I needed to marry a man who would keep me in the manner to which I would LIKE to become accustomed. He could have put it more simply and just pointed out that I have champagne tastes and a beer budget, but, either way, unfortunately, I didn't marry a rich man and the result is that I watch my rands and cents when I buy wine. This is absolutely not a problem at all if you are just introducing yourself to red wines, because all the best starter reds, in my opinion, are cheerfully cheap. If you pay a lot of money for a red wine, you can reasonably expect that the cost takes into consideration one or more of the following factors:

((◦ Lots of new oak

((◦ Lots of super-concentrated fruit, probably from low-yielding vines (more on this later)

- ◖ Lots of tannin and/or alcohol
- ◖ Lots of marketing hype
- ◖ And probably a ridiculously heavy bottle as well

If you're starting out experimenting with red wines for the first time, you don't want any of these things anyway, so let price be your guide and go for cheaper wines with only a hint of oak, that have soft, juicy fruit and easy levels of tannins. We can leave the others for later as your tastes develop.

OLD VINES/YOUNG VINES OR HIGH YIELDS/LOW YIELDS?

You'll often hear winemakers trying to talk up their wines by informing you that they come from old vines or that the yields are really low. When this happens, just nod sagely, as if that explains everything, come back here – and let's talk about sex.

The first thing to understand is that a vine's priority in life is different from ours. A vine wants to produce as many bunches of big, fat, juicy grapes as possible, in the hope that birds will eat them and then poo the seeds out all over the place, allowing the vine to have lots of little baby vines everywhere. The problem with this reproduction cycle is that if we let the vine produce tons of grapes, which obviously makes for lots of grape juice and therefore plenty of wine, the fruit often won't have much flavour.

So winemakers, who are more interested in quality than quantity, interfere with the vines and snip off some of the half-formed bunches of grapes before they really get going. This ensures that the flavours get shared among a smaller number of bunches, thereby making the fruit tastier. This is referred to as low yields, where the winemaker harvests a restricted amount of grapes from each hectare of land. The flip side is that because the winemaker loses half the grapes, she can make only half as much wine, which is one of the reasons some wines cost twice as much as others – to make up that shortfall.

LET'S TALK ABOUT SEX, BABY

The other factor that restricts the quantity of grapes grown is the age of the vines – this is an effect of nature and it is where we bring in the sex element. When you're young and keen, you're at it like a rabbit – bonking in the backs of cars, on your parents' sofa, in the doorways of hairdressers (oh, hang on, that might just be me) – lots of energy and drive, but not necessarily much – shall we say – finesse. As you get older, you don't have as much variety as before – work kicks in, you have sleepless nights with the kids, and all this means that you don't get round to having sex as much as you might wish. But when you do – the wonderfulness of familiarity, the excitement of confidence and the intimacy of being with someone you truly love means that sex, albeit infrequent, is more fabulous than it's ever been.

In a similar sort of way, young vines produce the equivalent of teenage-shagging grapes: plenty of them, but crap quality, whereas older ones are more George Clooney in style – fewer grapes, but more refined and far higher quality. And now excuse me while I go for a short lie down.

SOME WINES TO TRY

Right – back from the bedroom, fanning myself as I return. So, my best advice is, when trying red wines for the first time, go for inexpensive ones. That way, you should get fruit from younger vines. They will have less oak, less tannin and the overall experience is that these will be easy-drinking styles of wines. If you're still worried that these wines might taste bitter or nasty, then make sure you try them with food. A good pinch of salt on your meal will work wonders when it comes to smoothing out and soothing down a rampant tannin.

KLEINE ZALZE GAMAY NOIR

This grape variety is the one used in Beaujolais, in France, and it's the perfect variety for newcomers to red wine. Soft and juicy, with flavours of raspberry and strawberry.

OBIKWA SHIRAZ

This range of very entry-level wines can be a bit mixed quality-wise, but the Shiraz has always been a shining beacon of consistency, value, interest and soft, sweetish black fruit.

STELLENBOSCH HILLS POLKADRAAI PINOTAGE/MERLOT

A regular winner in good-value competitions and one of the easiest-drinking wines around. Lots of juicy, plummy fruit and a little hint of coffee, which is nice (if you like that kind of thing).

DIEMERSFONTEIN PINOTAGE

Many wine fundis loathe these chocolate/coffee-style wines, but I know that a lot of people enjoy them, and find the flavours pleasurable and the wines easy to drink. The distinctive chocolate/coffee flavours come from the oak used in making the wine and the best examples (of which this is one) combine these flavours with a good dollop of cherry/berry fruit.

AND WITH
FOOD

These are very versatile wines in terms of the food that they go well with. Personally, I like light reds with cold meats, charcuterie, a nice terrine or a good-old English pork pie. But if you want to try them with fish (maybe tuna) or chicken, you will also find they go well together. It's sometimes a good idea to think of the fruit flavours that you find in these sorts of wines (like strawberries, cranberries and cherries), and then seek out dishes that also feature these fruits or go well with them (e.g. duck and cherries, turkey and cranberries).

says David Finlayson of Edgebaston Wines

When I first met David Finlayson, he was just starting his own label, Edgebaston Wines, named after his mother's home town in the UK and the original name of his farm. My restaurant was one of the first to list his only wine at the time, then simply named 'Chardonnay'. How times have changed! Now David has a whole stable of yummy-sounding wines that give people a good idea of what's inside the bottle. Hence The Pepper Pot Shiraz really is as spicy as the name suggests, and The Berry Box bursts with ripe, red and black fruit.

So, unlike these examples, why don't most wine labels help you understand what the wine actually tastes like? David makes no bones about it: it's all the marketers' fault!

It's surprisingly difficult to write meaningful tasting notes and back labels for bottles of wine. And I know, because I've done it. You need to give information about the style of wine in the bottle, tell consumers a bit about how it's made and provide the information required by law, such as alcohol levels and origin of the wine. But you don't want to go over the top either. As David says, 'Not everyone who enjoys a glass or two of wine wants it to be a profound intellectual experience. Usually, they just want something to relax with.'

So, where should the technical information end and the storytelling begin? And where does it stop being simply telling the story of the wine and become bullshit? That's a big problem for David, who remarks, with feeling, 'If I read about one more wine that is redolent of the scent of wild flowers on a warm summer's day, I'm going to put that bouquet of flowers where the sun don't shine.' (Note to self – cancel that NetFlorist order now.)

I understand what David is saying about over-excitable marketing folk who delight in creating their own reality and painting ridiculous images of things that don't exist or have no relevance. But I think he forgets that he is a particularly erudite and lyrical advocate for his own wines, one who is perfectly capable of explaining his wines in picturesque, yet straightforward ways, whereas a lot of winemakers simply take refuge in noting the age of the barrels and throwing in technical terms such as 'malolactic fermentation', 'racking' and 'cold-stabilisation' without informing the poor consumer about what effect any of these things have on the wine.

On the whole, I think that some information is necessary, but telling the 'story' is the way to go. I have long held the opinion that people like to buy wines from people, and not factories, so stories are all-important. David says, 'I try to give the wine drinker an idea of what to expect in terms of flavour profile when they are going to drink the wine, hence The Pepper Pot is spicy, peppery, herbal and The Berry Box is all red berries and sweet dark fruits.' His attitude is 'why make life tougher for customers? If simplifying the equation in terms of name, but still delivering a mouthful of flavour, or stimulating the senses, instead of the grey matter, makes them happy, then that's great.'

And I am so with him on that.

If you stick your nose in a glass and get whiffs of damp cardboard, old mushrooms, wet laundry left overnight in the washing machine with the door closed, soggy wood – all of these should make you suspicious.

12

WINE FAULTS

IT'S EVERYONE'S WORST NIGHTMARE: YOU GET HOME AFTER A PIG OF A DAY, THE TRAFFIC WAS TERRIBLE, YOUR KID GOT DETENTION, THE CAT THREW UP ON THE CARPET. FINALLY, AFTER YOU HAVE MANAGED TO SORT EVERYTHING OUT, YOU HEAD FOR THE FRIDGE, POUR YOURSELF A GLASS OF WINE, SLUMP INTO YOUR FAVOURITE CHAIR ... AND THEN REALISE THAT WHAT IS IN YOUR GLASS HAS THE AROMA AND ATTRACTION OF A BABOON'S ARMPIT.

Yes, I'm afraid it's true. Sometimes, good wine goes bad and this can happen for various reasons. Here are a few of the more common problems and what you should do if they happen.

CORK DORK

I think the most common experience of wine spoilage is when a bottle is corked. Time was that a ridiculous number of bottles were ruined by being corked – as many as one in eight, according to some critics. Over time, however, the cork industry has cleaned up its act tremendously and has come up with better ways of manufacturing corks. And composite corks (little bits of cleaned cork pressed tightly into a cork shape) are definitely number one in many people's books.

What is a corked wine, anyway? It doesn't mean that the wine has small pieces of cork floating in it (that's just you being useless with the corkscrew), nor does it simply mean that the bottle is sealed with a cork. As one pourer behind the tasting table of an eminent winery once informed me, 'All our wines are corked.' When people say that a wine is corked, they mean it has become contaminated with an infection called trichloroanisole, or TCA. This occurs naturally in the bark of a cork tree (which is where corks come from) and if it makes its way into a bottle of wine, the TCA infection reacts with the flavour compounds of the wine and turns the wine sour.

HOW DO YOU RECOGNISE A CORKED WINE?

Generally by the smell. If you stick your nose in a glass and get whiffs of damp cardboard, old mushrooms, wet laundry left overnight in the washing machine with the door closed, soggy wood – all of these should make you suspicious. And if you decide to go ahead and taste it, you'll get bitter, green, woody, musty flavours, often with very little fruit. If this happens, then please, for the sake of the whole wine industry, take the bottle back to wherever you bought it. All winemakers will be very happy to replace it (the last thing they want is for you to think all their wine is crap, so they'd always prefer to give you a new, fresh bottle) and they will also be very keen to get their hands on the dodgy cork so they can beat up their supplier.

HOW TO RETURN A CORKED BOTTLE IN A RESTAURANT

I have some funny stories to tell about returning corked bottles in a restaurant. I've had waiters searching frantically through their stock, trying to find a bottle that isn't closed with a cork because they don't understand the term. I've also had someone try to open the replacement screwcap bottle with a corkscrew, which was particularly amusing to watch. But sometimes it can be a problem returning a corked wine in a restaurant because most of us don't want to make a scene and we're often afraid that people won't believe us. Sadly, there are not enough restaurants with staff who are capable of identifying a corked wine, so you need to stick to your guns if there appears to be nobody better qualified than you to make the call. Here's how to do it with the minimum of fuss.

Take your time with tasting the wine and, if you're not sure, tell your waiter you're going to leave it a few minutes to let it get some air and that he can come back later. While he's gone, swirl the hell out of the glass, give it lots of air and warm it up a little, especially if it's a white wine (when a wine is warmer, it reveals its flavours and aromas better). If you are now sure that the wine isn't right, then calmly, politely, but persistently, ask for another bottle. It's a bit of a stock-control issue for a restaurant but, ultimately, they have no reason to disbelieve you and can simply get the bottle replaced by the winery without loss. It's much better to take your time at the beginning and get it right than to drink half the bottle and then decide it doesn't taste good. Don't expect too much sympathy from the restaurant if you do that.

One last thing: people assume that a wine with a screwcap can't be corked because it hasn't been near a cork to pick up the infection. Wrong! Cork taint can be transferred into a wine in lots of ways – from a dirty barrel, tank or pipe in the cellar, or simply from the empty bottles before they are filled with wine. Granted, it's more unusual to encounter the problem in a screwcapped bottle, but if you get really strong smells and flavours of cork taint from a screwcapped bottle, you may well be right about your suspicion that the wine is corked – although you'll probably have a harder time persuading the waiter that you are.

OXIDISED WINES

Cork gets blamed for lots of faulty wine, and often people describe a wine as corked when in fact it has a different problem. One of the commonest faults is oxidation and the biggest culprit here is restaurants that serve wines by the glass. If you recall, in Chapter 7 we spoke about the effects that oxygen has on wine. Basically, it does the same thing to wine as it does to an apple cut in half: the oxygen causes the apple to go brown and start to rot. If a wine has an ill-fitting cork or a damaged screwcap, then oxygen can start this process without you being aware. How will you recognise an oxidised wine? It will probably be a little brownish in colour (or maybe just a darker gold if it's a white wine) and will smell of what people normally think of as sherry – sort of sweetish, a bit nutty, a bit raisiny, that kind of thing.

As I say, the most common incidents of oxidised wine occur in restaurants that serve wine by the glass. Don't get me wrong, I'm a big fan of by-the-glass wine in restaurants, but the fact remains that not everyone knows how to look after it properly. Once a bottle of wine has been opened, the oxidation process begins immediately. If you want to keep the bottle open for any length of time, you need to find a way to stop this, either by pumping the air out of the bottle and creating a vacuum, or by putting a protective layer of inert gas on top of the wine, preventing the oxygen reaching it. Even these measures, though, will extend its life by only a few days. The reality is that, generally, after four days most opened bottles of wine should be sent to the kitchen for cooking.

HOW TO SERVE WINE BY THE GLASS CORRECTLY

1. Use some kind of preservative system – a vacuum or otherwise – and repeat it every day once the bottle has been opened.
2. Keep opened wines in the fridge overnight – reds as well as whites – as this slows down oxidation.
3. Write the date you opened the wine on the label so you know how long it's been kicking around the bar.
4. Taste the wines by the glass every day to check they're still fine.

VOLATILE ACIDITY AND BRETTANOMYCES

Volatile acidity and brettanomyces are divisive subjects. Some people are able to tolerate – and even enjoy – low levels of these taints, and opinion is divided as to whether they even add value to some of the world's most famous wines.

Volatile acidity is caused by dodgy yeasts or bacteria that may be present during fermentation. It is most easily identified when the wine gives off a smell of vinegar or nail-polish remover. Brettanomyces, or 'brett', as most people refer to it, is a strain of yeast that is highly prized in beermaking. In wine, however, it produces a range of smells that range from the more delicately named 'farmyard' to the no-beating-about-the-bush 'horseshit'. A lot of wineries, particularly older cellars with older styles of winemaking, are prone to these infections (which can be avoided with a scrupulously clean cellar environment). At a low level, however, they can add complexity and interest (particularly brett). But if it's not your thing – send the bottle back.

There are lots of other types of infections and spoilages that can taint wine, but, hopefully, these are the main ones you'll come across. Happy nosing!

If you have deep pockets and an even deeper cellar, then put away a couple of cases and drink a bottle every year to see how the wine is developing. When you think it cannot possibly get any better, it blows your socks off and gives you a little wine orgasm in your mouth, then drink all the remaining bottles. Feel free to invite me along when you do.

13

FULL-BODIED RED WINES

BEING SOMEWHAT FULL-BODIED AND VOLUPTUOUS MYSELF, I ALWAYS ENJOY A BIG RED WINE.

Nearly all the world's most famous wines are big, bold reds – top Bordeauxs and Burgundies, expensive northern Italian and Spanish productions, meaty Aussie and Californian icons. Part of their charm and attraction is that these are the kinds of wines you really need to keep for a few years before you drink them.

Well, obviously you don't have to, but it may prove to be worth your while. When it comes to keeping wine for any length of time, the wine needs to contain one or more of the following naturally occurring preservatives:

((◐ Tannin

((◐ Sugar

((◐ Alcohol

((◐ Acidity

Of course, this isn't rocket science: we have been preserving foods (and less savoury things such as dead bodies too!) in acidic vinegar, sweet honey and alcohol for millennia, so we know these substances work. Tannin is less familiar to us as a preservative, but time and experience have proved that wine with a good tannic 'structure' stays fresh for longer. In fact, time is tannin's best friend because when a tannic wine is young, it can be unbearably dry and difficult to drink, so the process of preserving the wine, allowing the flavours to change and develop over time while keeping them fresh and interesting, also allows the tannins to evolve, making them softer and easier to drink.

The most important thing about keeping wine for any length of time is that it must be worth keeping in the first place. A wine can have all the tannin/

sugar/alcohol/acidity you like, but if it doesn't have enough fruit/concentration/character/interest, then you can cellar it till Judgement Day and it won't get any better. However, if it does have enough 'oomph' and 'va-va-voom' to make it worth hanging on to, the ageing process will allow the flavours to develop, the wine to become more complex and interesting, the tannins to soften and integrate into the wine, and, all in all, you should get a hell of a lot more drinking pleasure from it after those few years.

HOW LONG SHOULD I KEEP THIS BOTTLE OF WINE?

Ah – if only I had a rand for every time I'm asked that question ... There is no hard-and-fast rule but here are a few pointers to get you on the way.

HOW MUCH DID YOU PAY FOR IT?

With the very best will in the world, it is unlikely that any wine costing under R100 is going to have enough concentration and fruit to make it worth cellaring for too long. If you've paid even less than that, then the answer to 'How long should I keep it?' is probably 'lunchtime'. You get what you pay for in wine, and a more expensive wine should mean it comes from more concentrated, flavoursome grapes. Not always, perhaps, but often. So if you want it to be worth drinking in a decade, pay a decent amount for it now.

If you want to keep your wine, you need a good place in which to age it properly. And, despite what kitchen designers tell you, the absolute worst place of all is those horizontal slots in between your kitchen units, which are generally near the oven. This is a terrible idea because if you want to keep your wine in good condition, you must keep it in a cool, dark environment at a constant temperature. Anything else (by the oven, in direct sunlight, in fluctuating temperatures) will prematurely age your wine. If you haven't got anywhere suitable at home and you desperately want to store some wine, get in touch with a professional wine-storage agent, such as Wine Cellar, and ask them for help.

DO YOU ACTUALLY LIKE DRINKING OLDER WINES?

This isn't a facetious question. A lot of people keep wines for a long time because they think it's the thing to do, and are then terribly disappointed when they come to drink their vinous treasures because they hate the way they taste.

When a wine gets older, it loses all the upfront and in-your-face fruitiness that it starts out with, and in its place come what we call 'secondary' and even 'tertiary' flavours. These are flavours that emerge from the winemaking process itself – fermentation, lees contact, oak ageing. What starts out as a clean, citrusy Chardonnay with toasty oak may become a honeyed, nutty, baked, caramelised-fruit mouthful after a few years. If you like these more complex flavours, then go ahead and squirrel away your wine for decades. But if fresh, uncomplicated fruit is your thing, rather drink your wine now and be thankful you can save money on your air-conditioning costs.

The bottom line when it comes to answering the question, how long should I keep this wine? is that no one ever knows for sure. If you have deep pockets and an even deeper cellar, then put away a couple of cases and drink a bottle every year to see how the wine is developing. When you think it cannot possibly get any better, it blows your socks off and gives you a little wine orgasm in your mouth, then drink all the remaining bottles. Feel free to invite me along when you do.

FULL-BODIED AND VOLUPTUOUS

What gives a wine its body? Good question. Full-bodied wines are generally made from riper grapes, which have more sugar, which, in turn, translates into more alcohol. It's the combination of ripe fruit, possibly a tiny bit of residual sugar and higher alcohol that makes wines taste bigger, fatter and fuller in your mouth, coating every single taste bud and leaving you with a warm, fuzzy feeling as it slips down your throat.

When it comes to big reds, I think it's best to start with some single grape varieties before moving on to the big-gun blends, but it's really up to you.

TRY THESE

HARTENBERG MERLOT

It is whispered around the wine-rumour mill that South Africa isn't fab at making Merlot. Be that as it may, if you want to try a good example, then Hartenberg is where I would start. And after you've enjoyed this wine, move over to their range of excellent Shirazes as well.

WARWICK THE FIRST LADY CABERNET SAUVIGNON

Very good step-up wine for people who are used to lighter styles. This is serious enough to keep you interested, but not in any way scary, with plenty of soft fruit and pliable tannins.

DOMBEYA SHIRAZ

Elegant and ripe with rich hints of chocolate and perfume. Drink it or dab it on your wrists – either will work.

KWV ROODEBERG

Neglect this old favourite at your peril! This is a really good drinking wine that marries the softness and spice of Shiraz with the structure and juiciness of Cabernet, and all at an excellent price.

STELLEKAYA ORION

Lovely Bordeaux-style blend made from mainly Cabernet Sauvignon with some Merlot and other grapes. Chewy, dark and dense; add cheese or steak for best effect.

VILAFONTÉ SERIES C

There are two Vilafonté wines and this one generally has more Cabernet in it, hence the 'C'. It's a big, brooding monster that needs at least ten years before you should go near it. But when you do, it rewards you with complex flavours, similar to a top Bordeaux at its best.

MVEMVE RAATS DE COMPOSTELLA

Including this wine in this line-up is a personal indulgence, since I believe it pretty much sells out on release, so you probably can't find it. But if you want to try the finest red wine made in South Africa – bar none – get yourself on that pre-release list somehow, some way. You'll thank me for it.

Red wine with steak – that's the thing, isn't it? Yes, but contrary to popular opinion, the protein content of a steak isn't what helps to soften and smooth out the red-wine tannins. It's actually more to do with the salt most chefs use to season the meat before they cook it. But, in terms of strength of flavours, the robust, strong, meatiness of a steak will indeed be enhanced by a robust, strong, meaty red wine, so from that perspective it's a good pairing.

Salty cheeses also help soften a very tannic wine, but the flavours of most reds can clash with the pungency of a lot of cheeses, so this doesn't always work.

If you're not a red-meat eater, you need to find a way of balancing out these powerful red wines. Try hearty dishes using meaty veggies such as mushrooms or aubergines. Just watch out for tomato-based sauces, as they can be killers with red wines.

Building up your own cellar

by Mike Ratcliffe of Vilafonté

Most wineries release their wines as soon as they can, generally to help with cash flow, even if they're not quite ready to drink. Sadly, most of us don't have space to establish a wine cellar at home – I certainly don't – but if you want to drink your wines a little bit older, there is another option you can explore.

Vilafonté is a joint South African–US venture and, right from the start, it has made a big thing about keeping its wines for some time before releasing them to the market, as well as creating a 'wine library' of older vintages for their customers to buy. Mike Ratcliffe, Vilafonté's managing director, explains why they do this: 'We are seeing steady growth in demand and appreciation for well-cellared, older vintage wines. In particular, restaurants and other buyers around the world are slowly waking up to the fact that the top South African wines do get better with age. I believe that there is no great winery in the world that has achieved greatness without having the capacity to showcase its future by displaying its past.'

At the moment, 25 per cent of each vintage made of Vilafonté's two red wines is kept back for later release. Even though Vilafonté has now had ten years' experience of cellaring its wines, Mike still says it's not always easy deciding how long to keep the wines. They taste their reserve stock regularly and try to make the most informed recommendations to their customers. But, as Mike confesses, 'We don't really ever know. We make detailed notes and send them to our wine-club members annually with a recommendation to either drink or hold. Our members do pay attention to our suggestions, but we also see that too many of our wines are consumed too young as temptation kicks in.'

So, how do you avoid this temptation? Mike recommends that you work out how much money you've got to spend on wine per year and decide on a certain proportion – 10 per cent is a good figure – that can be spent on wines to be cellared: 'This means that you still have lots of wine to drink when temptation creeps up on you.' He also suggests that you keep a note of your purchases and the wines you have in your cellar, and the easiest way is to 'paste a simple white sticker onto each of your bottles and note when you bought it and the length of time that you would like to hold onto it as a minimum. This means that when you reach for the bottle, all the information is readily at hand.'

His final recommendation is that you spend a bit more than normal on wines you want to keep: 'If you pay peanuts, you will generally get monkeys, so you must be able to see the future in a young wine. We look for structure, integrity, balance, purity and, most importantly, concentration. If a young wine doesn't taste great, it will never taste great.'

Sage advice, indeed.

Pinotage was invented in a lab in the 1920s by a professor of viticulture. It's had a rocky history even in its home territory of South Africa, and certainly elsewhere, with numbers of people claiming to be 'anything but Pinotage' drinkers. But, gradually, as our knowledge of the grape has improved, people are making better and better versions.

14

BLACK GRAPES 101

WE'RE ABOUT TO HEAD AWAY FROM STILL WINES AND LOOK AT BUBBLIES, SWEET AND FORTIFIED WINES, BUT BEFORE WE DO, HERE'S A QUICK WRAP-UP OF THE MAJOR BLACK GRAPE VARIETIES USED IN SOUTH AFRICA TODAY.

CABERNET SAUVIGNON ('CAB-UR-NAY SEW-VIN-YON')

The King of Grapes. Well, I think so anyway. Interestingly enough, Cab Sauv's parent grapes are actually Cabernet Franc (a black grape) and our old fave white variety, Sauvignon Blanc, so you'll often find Cabs that have a whiff of leafiness to them. Cab Sauv is a top-quality grape, and is often used to up the classiness factor of lesser varieties. Flavours and aromas: blackcurrants, blackberries, cedar wood, cigar box, occasionally minty/herbal hints and even some black-olive tapenade meatiness.

MERLOT ('MURR-LOW')

The classic blending partner of Cab Sauv. These two grapes, plus Cabernet Franc, Malbec and Petit Verdot, form the basis of red wines from Bordeaux, in France. Hence, you may notice that similar combos in South Africa are referred to as Bordeaux blends. Merlot doesn't always do that well in South Africa, particularly at the cheaper end of the market, where it can make wines that taste like alcoholic jam, but good versions balance ripe fruit with soft tannins and good structure. Flavours: fatter, fleshier black fruits, like plums and blackberries, with hints of chocolate on the side.

CABERNET FRANC ('CAB-UR-NAY FRONK')

The Daddy of Cabernet Sauvignon, now outclassed by its more famous son. But hang on a minute – that's not entirely true, as Cab Franc is now growing in popularity (albeit slowly) and certainly growing in prestige as more and more winemakers become convinced that this grape can make better wines in South Africa than it does in France. I've been saying this for many years, so I sincerely hope it becomes accepted wisdom during my lifetime and I can garner fame and kudos for my farsightedness. Flavours: blackcurrants, blackberries, geranium leaves, lead pencils, fynbos.

SHIRAZ/SYRAH ('SHI-RAZZ'/'SIRRA')

These are just two different names for the exact same grape variety, and whether you label your wine as one or the other, it comes down to marketing preference and whichever name you think is going to appeal most to your customers. Shiraz is hugely successful in South Africa and makes some of the country's top wines, largely because we have a warm climate, which suits the variety. It originally comes from the Rhône Valley, in France, and people often refer to blends that include Shiraz as 'Rhône blends'. Flavours: black plums, black cherries, spices (especially pepper), some smoked meats; cooler-climate versions often show hints of perfumed violets.

PINOTAGE ('PEE-NO-TARZH')

This is South Africa's very own grape variety. Pinotage was invented in a lab in the 1920s by a professor of viticulture, Abraham Izak Perold. It's had a rocky history even in its home territory of South Africa, and certainly elsewhere, with numbers of people claiming to be 'anything but Pinotage' drinkers. But, gradually, as our knowledge of the grape has improved, people are making better and better versions. I used to hate this variety when I first came to South Africa about a decade ago, but now I really enjoy it – and I'm not alone. When other countries (Australia, the US and Israel, to name but a few) start planting your 'local is lekker' grape variety, you know you've arrived. Flavours: black cherries, plums, leather, spice, hints of smoke; sometimes can be made in a controversial (but popular) 'chocolate/coffee' style.

PINOT NOIR ('PEE-NO NWAR')

A fickle, fussy grape variety that is difficult to grow and awkward to make into wine. So, why do we bother with it? Because when it's good, it's soooo good you can forgive it everything. Needs a cooler climate and some may argue that South Africa is too hot for it to be really successful. But we keep trying because, you know, when it's good ... Flavours: red berries (strawberries and raspberries), Earl Grey tea, wet earth, sweet spices.

The following are some other black grape varieties you might come across:

RHÔNE GRAPES – GRENACHE NOIR, MOURVÈDRE, CARIGNAN, CINSAULT

To go along with a good dollop of Shiraz/Syrah, many winemakers add some of these grape varieties to make a Rhône-style blend. They are proving incredibly popular at all price levels and South Africans are relishing the freedom our wine laws allow and adding interesting tweaks of port varieties (see next paragraph), Cabernet Sauvignon and often Pinotage as well in these blends.

PORT GRAPES – TOURIGA NACIONAL, TEMPRANILLO, TINTA BAROCCA/ RORIZ/FRANCEZA

Traditionally, South Africa has made some of the finest fortified sweet wines outside Portugal, so we have plenty of these indigenous Portuguese grape varieties planted. As people go off fortified wines, however, canny winemakers, such as Boplaas and De Krans, are increasingly using them to make gutsy, hearty table red wines as well, often blending them with varieties such as Shiraz and Cabernet. Bring it on, say I.

Madame Lilly Bollinger: 'I drink champagne when I'm happy and when I'm sad. Sometimes I drink it when I'm alone. When I have company I consider it obligatory. I trifle with it if I'm not hungry and drink it when I am. Otherwise I never touch it – unless I'm thirsty.'

15

Wine tech | **NO. 6**

FIZZING IT UP

SOMETIMES I THINK EVERY WINE SHOULD BE FULL OF BUBBLES. I FREELY CONFESS TO BEING A CHAMPAGNE SLUT, A BOLLIE DOLLY, A BUBBLY QUEEN – WHATEVER UNFLATTERING TERM YOU CARE TO USE, IT NEVER BOTHERS ME, AS LONG AS THE BUBBLES KEEP POURING.

Sparkling wine is growing in popularity in South Africa and the rest of the world, so here are some hows and whys of fizz.

Anyone got a SodaStream? No, honestly, I'm not being facetious – that is definitely one way of putting bubbles into wine. All right, perhaps in the case of wine, it's done on a more commercial scale, but injecting carbon dioxide into a tank of wine is an efficient and inexpensive way of making many a party fizz. If you're going to have your bubbly in a cocktail such as a Buck's Fizz, a carbonated wine is a good, inexpensive option.

The best way of creating the bubbles, however, is to start a second fermentation. Do you remember the equation in Chapter 2: sugar + yeast = alcohol + CO_2? With the wines we have looked at so far, we've ignored the CO_2 part, and the gas has simply disappeared off to ruin the ozone layer, but when it comes to making sparkling wine, the gas now becomes an all-important element of the wine.

Basically, with sparkling wine, two fermentations take place. The first fermentation produces a normal dry wine with no bubbles because the carbon dioxide disappears, as usual in winemaking. But once you have this base wine, as it is called, a little more sugar and yeast are then added and, this time, the fermentation container is sealed. What happens next? The yeast eats the sugar (as we know), slightly increases the alcohol, as per the equation above, and produces more carbon dioxide. However, because this time the fermentation container is closed, the bubbles can no longer escape into the atmosphere, and become trapped and absorbed in the wine. Ta-da! The result: bubbly wine.

TO LEES OR NOT TO LEES?

When making fizz, the containers used for this second fermentation can be either large sealed tanks or individual bottles. The bottle-fermentation method is the one used to produce champagne. And while we're on the subject, did you know that you can call a wine champagne only if it comes from the Champagne region of France? People in South Africa sometimes refer to our bottle-fermented wines as 'champagnes', but actually, that's wrong. South African bottle-fermented sparkling wines are called Méthode Cap Classique, or MCC; in Spain they are called Cava and all the best sparkling wines in the world are made this way. Making a bubbly wine in a tank is a much cheaper method, mainly because you can remove it from the lees and clean it up more easily in bulk.

What are lees? When the yeast has done its work, chowed all the sugar and turned it into alcohol and CO_2, it then dies because there's nothing left for it to eat. The dead yeast cells fall to the bottom of the tank forming a sediment known as 'lees'. The lees can impart a lot of flavour, so some winemakers use them to give their wines extra intensity, stirring up the tanks and rolling their barrels around to get the flavour thoroughly incorporated into the wine. Lees contact is what gives the best sparkling wines their distinctive yeasty/bready/salty character, which is highly prized by aficionados. If you don't like those tangy flavours, then your best bet is a carbonated or tank-fermented sparkling wine because they generally have less of this yeastiness.

The lees now need to be removed before the wine can be sold, otherwise the wine would be murky. If the second fermentation is done in a tank, then it's a straightforward process to filter out the lees and bottle the crystal-clear wine while keeping it under pressure so that the bubbles are retained.

TRADITIONAL AND STILL THE BEST

There is no legislation about how long you must leave your wine in the tank with the lees before you bottle it, but there is a great deal of legislation around the best method of making sparkling wine – the traditional ('champagne') or MCC method, where the second fermentation takes place in the bottle. The process is basically the same as the tank method up to a point. The still wine is put in bottles with a little extra sugar and yeast, and a crown cap (like the ones used to seal beer bottles) is put on, locking in the carbon dioxide. This bottle now becomes the fermentation container. The second fermentation takes place and then the yeast dies when it has eaten all the sugar.

The wine must then stay in contact with the lees for a minimum period (in South Africa it's nine months but that is about to be increased to twelve months) to give those tangy, yeasty flavours. Some premium wines will be aged on the lees for up to five years, and sometimes even longer, making them intensely flavoursome and rich. When the winemaker is satisfied with the level of yeastiness, he or she carries out two different processes called riddling and disgorging to remove the lees and make the wine clear and gunk-free, ready for sale.

RIDDLING AND DISGORGING

While the second fermentation takes place, the bottle of wine is lying on its side and as the yeast cells die, they form a layer of sediment running the length of the underside of the bottle. The task now facing the winemaker is to get this mucky stuff down to the neck of the bottle, ready to be removed – this is known as riddling. Slowly, gently and over a period of time, each bottle is twisted round (to loosen the sticky lees) and then tilted a little, twisted and tilted a little more, twisted and tilted still more, until all the sediment has been slowly shifted into the neck of the bottle and rests against the crown cap, and the bottle itself is now standing neck down in a vertical position.

When the lees are in place, it's time for disgorging. The neck of the bottle is dipped in a tank of freezing dry ice or carbon dioxide and the dollop of lees is frozen into a solid pellet. The bottle is quickly flipped upright, the crown cap is removed, the frozen pellet of gunk is propelled out of the bottle with a resounding 'ping' (it's forced out by the pressure of the gas inside the bottle), then the sweetness is quickly adjusted before the cork is inserted, the wire cage is tied on to hold it in place and the wine goes for another little lie down before it is labelled and sold: riddled, disgorged, clean and ready to drink.

I could wax lyrical for hours about fizz, telling you lots of interesting facts, debunking lots of myths and, of course, drinking plenty of it on the way. More of that in the next chapter, but for now, here is my favourite quote from my favourite Champagne lady, Madame Lilly Bollinger: 'I drink champagne when I'm happy and when I'm sad. Sometimes I drink it when I'm alone. When I have company I consider it obligatory. I trifle with it if I'm not hungry and drink it when I am. Otherwise I never touch it – unless I'm thirsty.'

What a heroine! That's my type of fizz drinker.

After all, is there anyone who would dare propose to their fiancée

without its help or celebrate a special occasion without a bottle or

more of bubbly?

16

SPARKLING WINES

NOW I COME TO THINK ABOUT IT, I COULD HAVE WRITTEN EVERYTHING IN THIS BOOK AGAIN, BUT THIS TIME TALKING ONLY ABOUT SPARKLING WINES.

Because there is a massive range of styles, colours, sweetness levels – and quality levels – in sparkling wines, the whole range of topics we've looked at so far could certainly be covered again just for bubbles. Instead, though, here are a few of the essential things that will help you decipher what's inside a bottle of sparkling wine.

We're used to thinking of fizz as being either white or pink but, actually, there are increasing numbers of wineries that make sparkling red wines as well. I have to confess that I am not a fan of fizzy red – it plays with my head to chill a red wine to the level needed in order to control the bubbles. And when you chill it to that level, it makes the tannins very bitter (see Chapter 10 for more details on tannins). So, sorry to all you sparkling-Shiraz producers – you're the only fizz that I'm happy to leave.

The classic grape varieties used to produce champagne (and most of the best sparkling wines in the world) are Chardonnay (a white grape) and two black grapes – Pinot Noir and Pinot Meunier. In South Africa, we also use a lot of Chenin Blanc (because we grow a lot of Chenin Blanc), as well as Pinotage and sometimes other grapes too. If you want to make a white fizz, you can still use black grapes, just remove the skins before they can add any colour. If you want to make a pink fizz, then either allow a little bit of skin contact or simply mix some red wine into your white wine. If your wine is made solely from white grapes, it may be called 'blanc de blancs' on the label, meaning a white wine from white grapes. If it is made just from black grapes, it may say 'blanc de noirs', and this term is used for both white and rosé wine.

Most sparkling wines are made as dry wines (except for those that get SodaStreamed, which are more often than not sweet) and then, just as they are bottled, nearly all of them have the sugar level adjusted by the addition of some sweet grape juice just before the cork is inserted. This technique is called 'dosage' and can make sparkling wines anything from 'sec' (moderately or fairly dry), 'demi-sec' (off-dry), 'semi-sweet' or 'doux' (sweet). The most common word on bottle-fermented fizzes is 'brut' ('unequivocally dry' in French), but you will sometimes see wines labelled as 'brut nature' or 'brut zero'. In these cases, there has been no 'dosage' sugar added, and the wine will be teeth-tinglingly dry, with a yummy, fresh, salty tang.

VINTAGE OR NON-VINTAGE?

A wine has a vintage, or year, on the bottle if all the grapes used to make it were picked in a single year. When it comes to still wines, a vintage is considered a better-quality wine, and non-vintage or 'NV' is usually regarded as a term for cheaper, generic wines. However, this is not the case with fizz. There is much hype surrounding the top champagne brands and, for that matter, the top MCC (Méthode Cap Classique) brands as well. A large proportion of the price we pay for these wines goes on maintaining this hype and marketing them as aspirational 'accessories'. It is therefore crucial that there is no variation in quality from one vintage to the next, so that the winery can maintain its ongoing brand value in the market.

Winemakers achieve consistency by blending sparkling wines from different years. The wines from previous years are called reserve wines and sometimes they will spend time in oak barrels, giving the winemaker even more options to achieve consistent results every time. So, as you can imagine, the best bubbly houses try and retain their winemakers for as long as possible, because there is no recipe to this blending process – it's all to do with taste and experience gained over the years.

A FEW FIZZ MYTHS DEBUNKED

You have to hand it to the fizz marketers: they've done a darned fine job of creating mystique, allure, sexiness and excitement about a bottle of carbonated alcoholic liquid. After all, is there anyone who would dare propose to their fiancée without its help or celebrate a special occasion without a bottle or more? And part of their 'creating their own reality' has been to propound and perpetuate a number of myths about everyone's favourite bubbles. So, here are a few truths to set the record straight.

MYTH 1 A sparkling wine cannot be corked

Incorrect: the bubbles give the wine no protection from cork taint. This infection, which also affects sparkling wine, is called trichloroanisole, or TCA for short and it makes the wine taste dull, like wet cardboard, damp cupboards and mouldy mushrooms. Check out Chapter 12 for wine faults.

MYTH 2 Dom Pérignon invented champagne

Sorry to bust this myth for you, but he actually spent his entire life trying to get rid of the bubbles from his wine. He should be credited instead with learning about blending different grape varieties and realising that 1 + 1 = 3, which is the basis of all great wines.

MYTH 3 A teaspoon inserted into an open bottle preserves the bubbles

What utter crap! I have no idea where this comes from and in my very vast drinking experience, it has never worked. Mind you, I don't often leave fizz open for more than an hour anyway, so I'm not an expert on this. ☺

MYTH 4   The 'coupe' (a shallow champagne glass) was modelled on Marie Antoinette's breast

Well, it's a good excuse for a few titters (as it were), but, despite every schoolboy's lurid hopes, it isn't true. The coupe was first used as a wine glass in the 1670s in England – some 80 years before Marie Antoinette was born in 1755. It wasn't modelled on any other famous buxom wenches either, I'm afraid, it's just a story that too many imaginative men would like to be true!

Sparkling wines come at all price levels; the price they sell for depends a lot on how they are made. Here are a few to try.

Inexpensive carbonated (SodaStreamed) sparkling wines:
NEDERBURG PREMIÈRE CUVÉE BRUT
Dry fizz made from Cape Riesling and Chenin Blanc. Fairly fruity, easy to drink and a good-value crowd-pleaser.

ROBERTSON WINERY SWEET ROSÉ
Sweetly pretty in pink, this is a good entry-level wine for people who don't like weird stuff like yeastiness and acidity. Frothy and fun.

Top-class bottle-fermented (MCC) sparkling wines:
SIMONSIG KAAPSE VONKEL
The original MCC, this has been setting the standard for Cape fizz for over 40 years now and is a crisp, fruity, yeasty mouthful with bubbles that dance on your tongue.

J.C. LE ROUX SCINTILLA
People often think that J.C. only makes inexpensive, carbonated sparklers. But, trust me, this flagship wine is one of South Africa's finest and best-

value fizzes. It cleans up at most MCC competitions and continues to offer wonderful depth, tangy citrus and delicious brioche flavours, and elegant bubbles.

VILLIERA MONRO BRUT

One of the Cape's finest fizz makers, Villiera has about eight versions in its stable, ranging from the well-known Tradition up to this one – its flagship fizz. The base wine is barrel-fermented before the fizz spends four years on the lees. Rich, savoury and utterly delicious.

GRAHAM BECK BLANC DE BLANCS BRUT

My favourite from the prestigious Graham Beck range of fizzes, and one that shows well every single year. Made from Chardonnay, some of it barrel-fermented, this is elegance in a bottle.

PIERRE JOURDAN BELLE ROSE

Enduringly popular range of bubbles from Haute Cabrière (these wines are bottled under the Pierre Jourdan name because that's how fizz is labelled in France – French tradition often uses the name of the original owner). Made from Pinot Noir, this wine is all about the fruit – fresh strawberries and raspberries with some almond notes.

AND WITH FOOD

Some mad individuals believe that fizz should be drunk only as an aperitif – more fool them, if you ask me. I was once at a Bollinger dinner where we drank a different Bollie with every course, including foie gras, steak and raspberries. Fizz is especially good with seafood because it has high acidity, so it can match the lemony citrus flavours, and always seems to go well with oysters and smoked salmon, and the like. But I've also had fizz very successfully with creamy pasta and cheese, and don't forget that the off-dry or sweet styles are wonderful with light, fruity puds like pavlova.

Try it with anything and, whatever you do, don't think you have to keep it for a special occasion. Fish and chips or scrambled eggs on toast on a cold Tuesday night in winter – perfect excuses to open a bottle of fizz.

MCC: Your everyday drink

says Pieter Ferreira of Graham Beck

'Should we drink MCC on special occasions only or every day? Is this even a question?' asks Graham Beck's cellarmaster and fizz fanatic, Pieter 'Bubbles' Ferreira. He's spent more than 30 years putting bubbles into bottles at some of the country's top MCC houses and, since MCC is a growing category both in Africa and the rest of the world, he is more than partly responsible for encouraging us all to break away from that once-a-year, special-occasion mentality and, in particular, getting us all to enjoy our fizz with food. 'Bubbly with food is a great combination and pairing is easy. People used to keep it for celebrations, but it has become more of a lifestyle drink. This means that when you have good company and good food, go with bubbles.'

As I mentioned above, the first MCC in South Africa was made by Simonsig in 1971. Twenty-one years later, Pieter was present at the founding of the Cap Classique Association, of which he is now the president, and is actively involved in driving standards in the industry ever upwards. The founding of the association was 'an event that took place in Swaziland, of all places, with Jeff Grier from Villiera. A cork from one of Jeff's magnums shot off, hit the ceiling and smacked esteemed wine critic Michael Fridjhon in the eye.' Possibly not the best way to get great reviews, but it hasn't deterred Pieter or Graham Beck's rise to fame and fortune.

With his bubblies drunk by celebs both real and fictional (the Obamas and James Bond are among his many fans), Pieter is adept at combining drinking fizz with his love of a good tale and a fantastic sense of show-manship. For him, Achim von Arnim of Haute Cabrière will always be the 'King of Sabrage' (sabrage is the art of lopping off the neck of an MCC bottle with a big sabre) and it was while Pieter was learning his trade with Achim in the 1980s that he made his first, successful attempt at this. Ken Forrester later taught him to expand his 'sabraging' repertoire by showing him how to do it using a teaspoon. 'Nowadays,' says Pieter, 'we sabrage with a champagne flute. I've opened many bottles like this and to date have broken the stems off only three glasses.'

For someone who spends so much of his time producing such a glamor-ous, luxurious and decadent product, Pieter is incredibly down to earth about his bubblies, valuing each one without being snobby or partisan. 'I often get asked which is my favourite bubbly and I always answer, the one in my glass right now!' Not that he's going to be silly and spray it all over the place like a Grand Prix winner or anything: 'What a waste of good bubbles!' he says. 'I would far rather drink it.'

Oh all right, Pieter, if you insist.

Hairy, frizzled-up berries covered in mould – sounds appetising? No, well it's one of those occasions when you must just close your mind and open your mouth. And I bet you didn't expect to find a comment like THAT in a wine book, did you?

17

SWEETS FOR MY SWEET, SUGAR FOR MY HONEY

BACK TO THE SWEET STUFF AGAIN. KIND OF FEELS LIKE WE'VE COME FULL CIRCLE HERE, DOESN'T IT?

Yet, for many newbie wine drinkers, although the idea of a full-on sweet dessert wine sounds appealing, it's probably the last style of wine they'll ever try.

Why is that? Two reasons, I'd say:

- ((Dessert wines are often more expensive, particularly when you factor in that they come in smaller bottles.
- ((Who the hell drinks dessert wines these days anyway?

Sad but true, I'm afraid, and people are missing out on some of the finest wines South Africa has to offer. Before we get onto some examples in the next chapter, how are these delicious, luscious, sticky dessert wines actually made in the first place?

JUST A SPOONFUL OF SUGAR ...

No, not really. Well, not in the best ones, anyway. Sweet wine is sweet because there is sugar present – we know that from earlier chapters. With dessert wines, mostly, this isn't added sugar though. Instead, dessert wines are made from grapes that are so concentrated and high in naturally occurring sugars that the yeast basically says, 'That's it. I give up. Can't do this, can't turn all that sugar into alcohol, far too much like hard work, just going to die instead.' And then it does. With the result that there is lots of residual sugar left over unfermented, so the wine remains sweet.

But how are the grapes so sweet and concentrated in the first place? There are several ways in which you can increase the sugar in the grapes:

1. Harvest them late. If you leave them on the vines for a very long time, grapes will carry on building up sugars in the sunshine until they are super-ripe and sweet. Generally labelled in South Africa as 'late harvest' or 'special late harvest', some are also labelled 'natural sweet'.

2. Dry them out. If you pick whole bunches of grapes and then lay them gently out on straw mats in the sun, it will dry them out and start turning them into raisins with concentrated sugars. Alternatively, you can pinch and damage the stems while the bunches of grapes are still on the vine, thus preventing water getting to them and causing them to dry out, or desiccate, in situ. These styles are usually labelled as 'straw wine', although sometimes winemakers use the French term 'vin de paille'.

3. Hope they attract a most glorious and fabulous fungus called noble rot. Not that I'm biased, but the best way of making a sweet wine by far is to pray that your wine gets infected with Botrytis cinerea ('bo-try-tus sinner-ear'), or noble rot, as it is more commonly known. This infection causes water to leach out of each grape without breaking the skin. The juice inside stays healthy – it just becomes increasingly sweeter as the water diminishes. The grapes are then picked very carefully, squeezed oh-so-gently and the resulting grape juice is so thick and concentrated with sugar that there isn't a hope in hell of the yeast managing to convert it all to alcohol.

The rot also gives the wines the most delicious flavours and aromas. For me, it always reminds me of my grandmother's furniture (some beeswax, a bit of dust and some of her perfume) but conventional wisdom says rye bread, honey, apricots and marmalade. Famous wines with noble rot? Sauternes in Bordeaux, France (the best-known example from that region being Château d'Yquem), Tokaji from Hungary, and Beerenauslese and Trockenbeerenauslese from Germany. Plus, of course, all our fabulous South African wines that are labelled as 'noble late harvest'.

It has to be said that if people saw the grapes used to make these dessert wines, they would drink even less of them than they do now. Hairy, frizzled-up berries covered in mould – sounds appetising? No, well it's one of those occasions when you must just close your mind and open your mouth. And I bet you didn't expect to find a comment like THAT in a wine book, did you?

The key, in my humble opinion, is knowing how and when to serve

dessert wines.

18

SWEET DESSERT WINES

HERE ARE FIVE REASONS WHY WE DON'T DRINK ENOUGH OF THEM:

---

1. Price

They seem expensive but, if you think about how many grapes you need to use to make one bottle (generally, you need almost 2 kg of noble-rot-infected grapes, as opposed to the normal 1 kg to one bottle), it kind of makes sense. Not that most people care if it makes sense: either it's expensive and they don't buy it, or it's not, and then they probably don't buy it anyway (see all the other reasons).

2. Badly served in restaurants

If you get dessert wine by the glass in a restaurant, then chances are that it was opened around three months earlier and is now a sticky, oxidised mess. Also, people serve dessert wines in ridiculously small glasses, which don't do them any favours. And, finally, they serve them at the wrong temperature – sweet wines need to be served ice cold. Staff training needed!

3. Never top of mind

I once had an open half-bottle of Sauternes in my fridge for a month and every time I opened the door, I thought to myself, 'Oh, I must drink that.' And every time I ate something that would have actually gone well with it, I completely forgot about it and drank something else instead. And how many waiters remember to offer you a glass with your dessert? It'll be a cold day in hell before you count more than two in anyone's lifetime.

4. Calories

This reason for not drinking dessert wine is a bit daft really, but I have heard plenty of people say they don't drink sweet wine because of the calories in the sugar. But then they go and heft down two bottles of something dry. Yes, there is sugar, but for the small glassful you're going to drink, it's probably fewer kilojoules than that bottle of Brut Zero fizz, which you're quite happy to knock back in its entirety. Just saying ...

5. Weirdness factor

Dessert wines are often made from unfamiliar grape varieties like Riesling and Semillon (unfamiliar to most, maybe, but not to you, now you've got this far in this book). They also have weird terms on the label like 'botrytis' and 'noble rot'. They have weird flavours and smells, like old churches, incense, dusty furniture and even sometimes petrol. This is just all too much – I'll have another glass of Sauvignon Blanc, please.

GET MORE THAN YOUR JUST 'DESSERTS'

The key, in my humble opinion, is knowing how and when to serve dessert wines. Firstly, they must be served from an ice-cold fridge and finished within three or four days, because they oxidise like other wines. Secondly, they must be served in a good-sized glass, so that the wine comes up to about halfway or less. Thirdly, they must be served with food. 'Well, duh, obviously!' I hear you cry. 'Hello, these are DESSERT wines – don't you think that's a bit of a clue?' Yes, thank you sarky-pants, I know that serving them with desserts is a good idea, but there is more to life than pudding. Dessert wines are also classic matches with two other foods – blue cheese and smooth liver pâtés. The almost metallic flavours and sharp pungency of a blue cheese are softened and tempered by sweetness, while the incredible richness of a cream-laden chicken-, duck- or goose-liver parfait is successfully brought into balance by the acidity of the best botrytised wines. So, don't go thinking you have to wait for dessert to drink your dessert wines, you can start the evening on them too and that way you can finish the whole bottle in one go.

Here are a few excellent examples to tempt your sweet tooth:

TRY THESE

FLEUR DU CAP NOBLE LATE HARVEST

This has won Platter five-star gongs for seven years in a row, so it really doesn't get much better than this. It also has fairly light botrytis flavours, so if the thought of drinking rotten grapes is freaking you out, then try this one first.

ORANGE RIVER CELLARS STRAW WINE

You want a good-value sweetie? This is your darling. From the vast, value-laden cellars of the Northern Cape comes this delicious dried-out-grape dessert wine. Great with cheese.

DELHEIM EDELSPATZ

A reliable favourite with lots of refreshing acidity offsetting the sweet, ripe apricots, oranges and almonds. Usually made from Riesling and often quite low in alcohol as well.

Learning to love your sommelier

by Xolani Mancotywa

Winemakers' noses are slightly out of joint at the moment. Why is that? Move over – because the new rock stars of the wine world, the sommeliers, are coming through. What is a sommelier? Someone who manages the wine cellar for a restaurant and is on hand to give guests advice about which will be the best wine for them to choose with their food is a general description but, actually, it's a lot more than that. It's a delicate balancing act, involving a lot of factors, according to Xolani Mancotywa, South African wine fundi and now a sommelier.

A lot of people have a fear of sommeliers, mainly because they are worried that they will be pressurised into ordering an expensive wine that they may not want. Xolani agrees: 'That certainly is the general impression. Sommeliers arrive at your table looking dapper in their tailor-made suits and with their big, fancy words that confuse the issue. As South Africans, we need to keep it simple, and the way to do that is to read your guests and find out what they like and what they normally drink.'

Yes, the sommelier does have a responsibility to try to sell good wines. 'The most expensive bottle I ever sold was a 1990 Château Latour for R87 000. A very well-behaved 24-year-old!' laughs Xolani. However, the main role of a sommelier is to 'make the guests comfortable, educate them and take them on a food-and-beverage experience. Should that fall short, we have failed you as a patron.'

What it really boils down to is that when you go out for a meal, you have already assigned responsibility for the food you're going to eat to your waiter and the chef, so why not hand over responsibility for choosing the wine as well? Most somms, as they're affectionately known, have gone through a lot of training before they dare use the title. Xolani holds the internationally recognised Court of Master Sommeliers Certificate, as well as his Wine & Spirit Education Trust (WSET) Level 3. He also holds a separate WSET qualification in spirits because, increasingly, somms should be able to advise you on spirits, cocktails, craft beers, coffees and even teas – if it's a beverage, your somm should know about it. But you don't need to take his every pronouncement as gospel and if there is a problem with the art of wine service, it's that it's not flexible enough, according to Xolani. He says, 'If you buy a bottle of white wine as a guest and you want to put ice in the glass, go ahead. The snobbery of judging this act must stop. What is wrong with it? You paid for it and if that's how we can enhance your experience, so be it. Wine-service professionals must listen more to what the guest chooses, as opposed to what we, as sommeliers, think is the textbook way of doing it.'

At the end of the day, wine snobbery is a two-way street and although sommeliers might strive to demystify wine without dumbing it down, customers need to learn how not to be afraid to say they don't know stuff. 'I recently had a customer who pointed to an Australian Pinot Noir on the wine list and asked for the white version,' says Xolani. 'We agreed to just go with another wine at the end of the day.'

That's good wine service and hospitality for you – and why we need to learn to love our somms.

Fortifying means to make something stronger, so if we fortify our houses, we put up electric fences, install security gates and buy a Rottweiler. And if we fortify our wines, we add some extra alcohol – generally grape brandy of some kind – raising the alcohol level to around 15–20 per cent.

19

PUTTING THE 'OOMPH' IN FORTIFIED WINES

I STRONGLY SUSPECT THAT IF YOU ARE GOING TO SKIP A CHAPTER IN THIS BOOK, IT WILL PROBABLY BE THIS ONE. WHO DRINKS FORTIFIED WINES THESE DAYS? YOU MAY ASK. AREN'T THESE THE DRINKS OF OUR GRANDPARENTS – OLD-FASHIONED AND UNTRENDY, POURED FROM BOTTLES THAT HAVE BEEN KEPT FOR TOO LONG AND SERVED IN IRRITATINGLY SMALL GLASSES? NO, FORTIFIED WINES ARE DEFINITELY NOT THE IN DRINK FOR MOST PEOPLE, SO SHOULD WE STILL BOTHER WITH THEM? IS THERE HOPE FOR FORTIFIED WINES? OR SHOULD THEY GO THE WAY OF PEPSI BLUE AND BECOME EXTINCT?

I am resoundingly in support of these types of wines, but before I go in to bat for fortified wine, let's just look at what types of drinks they are in the first place. Fortifying means to make something stronger, so if we fortify our houses, we put up electric fences, install security gates and buy a Rottweiler. And if we fortify our wines, we add some extra alcohol – generally grape brandy of some kind – raising the alcohol level to around 15–20 per cent.

The most important consideration is the point at which the fortifying process is done. If extra alcohol is added to dry wines when the fermentation has finished, then the fortified wine will obviously be dry, even if we might then add some sweetness later. An example is sherry, which always starts out as a dry wine. If, however, we kill the yeast halfway through doing its job of eating the sugar and converting it into alcohol, then we will have a sweet wine, because there will be some sugar left unchowed. The extra alcohol added to fortify a wine is what kills the yeast because it can't survive once the alcohol level gets too high. Therefore, wines made this way will be sweet, like ports.

UNDERSTANDING THE LABELS:
THE DIFFERENT STYLES OF FORTIFIED WINES

Firstly, in South Africa it is illegal to label ports as 'port' and sherries as 'sherry'. Port is an area-specific wine (the area in this case being the Douro Valley, in Portugal) and the Portuguese are protective about the trade name, so, since 2012, South African producers have had to remove the word 'port' from all wine made in that style.

Sherry is also an area-specific wine that originates from the southern tip of Spain, near the city of Jerez, and the same rules preventing its use have been in place for even longer than those banning the use of the word 'port' outside of the area. Most South African port producers describe the style of wine and add the word 'Cape' in front of it, hence 'Cape Ruby', 'Cape Vintage' and so forth. South African sherries are referred to as 'Pale dry' or 'Full cream', or similar.

What can we expect from the various types of port wines?

Cape Ruby

A dark-red, sweet, fresh-fruited wine, perhaps with some raisin and fruit-cake flavours. Easy-drinking, soft tannins, excellent value (for the most part), perfect with cheese or chocolate puds.

Cape Tawny

This is an underrated and under-drunk style. Pretty golden-brown colour with sweet flavours of nuts, caramel, toffee and hints of coffee. Serve it chilled, either with tangy cheeses or sip as an aperitif.

Cape Vintage

We tend to drink these far too early. Vintage port-style wines are concentrated, dark, brooding monsters that should be cellared away for at least ten years before we touch them. Lots of dried blackberries and spices, and – if you leave it long enough – silky tannins.

Cape Pink and Cape White

These styles of port are a little out of the normal, but there are a few available. They are sweet and fruity, and the best way to drink them is as a cocktail – add some ice, lemon, tonic water, lemonade, mint leaves, that kind of thing.

I have to confess to not being a fan of South African sherry, at least not dry ones. But South Africa does produce some excellent sweet sherries, which are fabulous with cheese or soup, or sipped on their own.

Fino
Technically, this means bone dry, pale in colour and yeasty. Well, it would be if it were a Spanish Fino. However, South African versions tend to be a little sweeter, with flavours of yeast, tangy olives and salt.

Cream
If you see this word on the label, whether it's 'Pale Cream', 'Medium Cream', 'Full Cream' or just 'Cream', then expect the wine to be sweet. Medium and Full Creams should be darker in colour, with flavours of nuts, toffee, caramel and honeyed raisins.

Muscadels and Jerepigos
These are some of the wines that will age the longest and are the most underrated South African wines – I've drunk 40-plus-year-old examples and they've been amazing. They are made from straight grape juice (Muscadels must be made with a Muscat variety, but Jerepigos can be made from anything – Pinotage, Chenin, Muscat and others.). The juice is then fortified with grape brandy. These are Cape specialities and if you can get your hands on some older versions from makers such as KWV and Nuy, they can be extraordinary.

If you were in Spain and ordered a sherry, the normal amount per person is a half-bottle and the normal glass used to serve it in is a tumbler or water glass. So don't think small – think big when it comes to fortified.

20

FORTIFIED WINES

SO – BACK TO THE QUESTION POSED IN THE PREVIOUS CHAPTER: WHY DON'T WE DRINK MORE FORTIFIED WINES AND SHOULD WE GIVE A DAMN ABOUT THEM ANYWAY? WELL, YES, I THINK WE SHOULD, ALTHOUGH MY REASONS ARE A CONFUSED MIXTURE OF NOSTALGIA, HISTORY AND PLEASURE.

The nostalgia bit is a rite of passage. The first alcohol that ever touched my lips was a tiny glass of sherry before Sunday lunch. I was probably about nine when my parents started letting me have the equivalent of a spoonful and probably about eleven when I started sneaking a refill out of the liquor cabinet without them noticing (by the way, I'm not suggesting at all that you should give alcohol to your children, I'm just saying how it was with me). It was a ritual, a treat, something out of the ordinary because growing up in the UK in the 1970s, we hardly ever had wine or beer in the house, so the one glass of sherry was my parents' entire intake of alcohol for the week. How times have changed! My parents now have a separate fridge for beer and wine, and, although they still tend to quaff the latter from boxes, and not bottles, at least there is a little more alcohol flowing than in the austere days of my childhood.

But back to the question of drinking fortified wines, I think there are three main reasons why we don't indulge in them sufficiently:

- They are perceived as old-fashioned and untrendy. 'Grandma's tipples' or old men with beards in gentlemen's clubs – those are seen as the people who drink port and sherry.
- They are served and stored *horrendously*. Sorry to shout, but really they are! Of course, no one is going to drink them if they are served in the poor condition I've come across at too many establishments. (More on this later.)
- There are a lot more choices of drinks available in terms of wine, spirits and other alcoholic drinks than there used to be.

The last point is never going to change, so there is nothing we can do about that. And, unless people suddenly allocate huge marketing budgets in an attempt to alter consumers' perceptions, I can't see anything changing about the first point soon either – certainly nobody has managed to any-where else in the world. But we can, and definitely should, do something about the second point. Here are some comments about serving fortified wines:

1. **No, you can't open them and continue to serve from that open bottle for the rest of the year.**

Just because they are fortified, doesn't mean they won't oxidise and go off. You should drink sherry within three weeks of opening the bottle, and port, Muscadel and Jerepigo within one month. All you grannies who drink one glass at Christmas each year should just drink more – 'cause life's too short to drink horrible, oxidised, rancid muck.

2. **Check the temperature.**

Pale, dry and Fino sherries should be served from the fridge, as should white and Tawny ports, white Muscadels and Jerepigos. If you haven't tasted a tangy, refreshing, ice-cold Fino before, then prepare to be amazed (actually – you'll probably hate it, as Fino is an acquired taste. But I urge you, please, to acquire it: you'll thank me for it later). Normal ports, and red Muscadels and Jerepigos should be served lightly chilled (i.e. at about 15–18 °C, otherwise the alcohol becomes too soupy).

3. Big glasses, please!

Is there anything more dispiriting than the teeny-tiny, horrible little glasses used to serve fortified wines? I hate, hate, hate those terrible schooner-shaped glasses, but even worse are those establishments that serve fortified wines in shot glasses, (yes really!) or the smallest possible wine glasses, filled to the brim with oxidised, sweet rubbish. If you were in Spain and ordered a sherry, the normal amount per person is a half-bottle and the normal glass used to serve it in is a tumbler or water glass. So don't think small – think big when it comes to fortified. Pour a generous portion into a decent-sized glass and let it breathe. So much concentration of flavour deserves nothing less.

4. A good Ruby is better than a bad young Vintage.

Not that I'm suggesting that the Vintage ports in South Africa are bad – far from it. But nobody gets any pleasure out of serving them too young – not the consumer, and certainly not the winemakers. Ten years old, in my humble opinion, folks. That's when we should start drinking our Vintage ports. This amount of ageing allows the tannins to soften, the alcohol to integrate and the flavours to fuse into an orgasmic mouthful of warm, spicy, dried fruit, Christmas cake and orange peel. And, in the meantime, we have utterly delicious Rubies and Tawnies to enjoy – far better to drink them instead.

The word on the street is that sherry bars are on the increase in the UK, and little birds tell me that they may become popular in South Africa as well. I'd like to think that a successful sherry bar would convert all non-fortified-wine drinkers to the strong stuff, but, in the meantime, if we can just concentrate on serving what we DO drink correctly, I think that would be a major step in the right direction. Try a few of these and see what you think.

TRY THESE

CALITZDORP CELLAR CAPE RUBY

Incredible-value port that is simply a pleasure to drink. Flavours of red and black berries; fresh and juicy with soft, ripe tannins.

BOPLAAS CAPE TAWNY

Rumour has it that this wine costs the producers more to make than they end up selling it for – but they keep on doing it because the patriarch of the family, Carel Nel, loves it so much. I love it too – nuts, toffee, apricots, figs.

DE KRANS CAPE VINTAGE

The Nel families of De Krans and Boplaas are 'fortified royalty' in this country and I could have picked almost any wines from their ranges. This is a regular five-star stunner, but please keep it until it's at least ten years after vintage. It will be worth it, I promise.

MONIS FULL CREAM
Generally, I'm a dry-sherry fan, but, in the absence of any good ones, I'll drink sweet. This is lovely – fairly similar in flavours to Tawny port but with a slight savoury edge to it. Great with French onion soup.

NUY RED MUSCADEL
The Kings of Muscadel! Year in, year out the trophies for this category are won by Christo Pienaar and his team at Nuy. Spicy, raisined delicious-ness in a bottle.

Forget the cheese, bring on the meat

says Margaux Nel of Boplaas Family Vineyards

I got a severe scolding from Margaux Nel, winemaker at Boplaas, when I suggested that fortified wines were an old-person's drink. 'This attitude from opinion formers, wine educators and show judges that fortified wines are lesser wines must stop now,' she said, 'otherwise South Africa will lose its richest heritage in winemaking terms.'

She may not be your idea of an average port drinker – being young, petite and pretty – but she's a formidable lady and if she says there is no reason why everybody, from every walk of life, shouldn't make fortified wines an everyday occurrence, then I, for one, am happy to believe her. Her vision of port-style wines is also fairly nostalgic, because, for Margaux, port and other fortified wines are liquid history, crafted in time-honoured ways, and they demonstrate the skill and passion of yester-year. These are styles of wines that we are very good at in South Africa and if we don't pass this enthusiasm on to the next generations, 'we might as well sit round our spittoons lamenting the passing of the "good-old days" until the end of time,' she says. And I tend to agree.

Serving fortified wines correctly is the key to their success, says Margaux, and she also believes that temperature is all important – many ports are served too warm. Unlike traditionalists, she thinks that port and cheese is boring and staid. Likewise, serving fortified wines with dessert gets the thumbs down as well: 'Don't let your port languish with some "heat 'n eat" malva pudding!' So what does she suggest instead as food matches for port? Well, child of the Karoo as she is, she recommends meat – and lots of it. Her suggestions include Wagyu ribeye with pomme frites and Cape Vintage Reserve; grass-fed beef-and-venison burger with caramelised onions and five-year-aged Cheddar with Cape Vintage; and slow-braised pork belly with dried apricot, prune-and-date stuffing (crispy crackling, and pumpkin-and-butternut purée are a must to accompany it) with chilled Cape Tawny.

All the exquisite dishes make me wish she lived around the corner and not 400 km away. Even the white ports, which she and her sister, Rozanne, usually drink as 'port tonics' with ice, lemon, mint and tonic water, are good with roast pork loin, a Sunday roast chicken or sole in a lemon-butter and parsley sauce. Who knew, eh?

So, the moral of this story is that fortifieds are fun and food-friendly – and we neglect them at our peril. Sure, Margaux is also experimenting with several delicious table wines from the port grape varieties, but those options can be explored to the full only if we keep South Africa's port heritage alive. Clearly, we all need to be creative in how we think about fortified wines and, perhaps, even in how we make them as well.

I suggested to Margaux that she could try some naked foot-stomping of the grapes, which is the traditional Portuguese way of making port. Although I don't think she took me seriously, that would definitely be one way to revitalise this segment of the industry, that's for sure!

This book doesn't tell you everything about wine (sorry – no refunds), but, instead, it should give you the confidence to go out and find out about wine for yourself. So, trust your taste, have faith in your abilities and believe that there are lots of different wines out there that you might also enjoy.

21

NOW WHAT?

If you started at the beginning and have made it this far, congratulations and I trust your liver isn't too sore. Hopefully, you've had some good wines on the way and have picked up the odd droplet of knowledge. So, what happens next? Where do we go from here? I'd like to reiterate what I said at the beginning of the book: the more you drink wine, the more you will learn about wine. If you're keen to go further on your journey into learning more about wine, here are some options you can try:

- Do a wine course. Unsurprisingly, I would recommend my internationally recognised Wine & Spirit Education Trust (WSET) courses, details of which you can find at www.thewinecentre.co.za, but there are plenty of others to choose from. Some are formal, others are more relaxed, but they are all a great excuse to meet up with like-minded boozers and try something new. Search online to find a course in your area.

- (⦿) Join a wine club. Some wine clubs have been established for many years; new ones are springing up all the time. Ask at your local wine shop if they know of any and if you can't find one you like, set up one yourself.

- (⦿) Go to tastings. A lot of wine retailers, hotels and restaurants offer tastings, ranging from free and informal ones to expensive gatherings featuring international wines, celebrated winemakers and delicious food. But they are all great opportunities to try something new and ask lots of questions – sometimes even to the winemakers.

- (⦿) Visit a wine farm. Admittedly, this is going to be somewhat easier if you live in the Western Cape, but if you do, or if you come down on holiday, then try make time to visit a few farms and, in particular, book yourself on a cellar tour. Seeing the equipment in situ makes a big difference in terms of understanding how wine is made.

- (⦿) Get online. Because wine is such a sociable thing, there are lots of websites, apps, Facebook groups and Twitter conversations you can tap into, which often include wine folk from around the world. I love the fact that I can ask questions on Twitter and have them answered by the people who made the stuff, by knowledgeable Masters of Wine or by some of the top journalists/movers/shakers who help shape this industry – how amazing is that?

◖◗ Try something different. My favourite quote from Mae West is, 'When faced with a choice between two evils, I always pick the one I've never tried before.' We've only skimmed the surface with this book and your new favourite wine is out there, somewhere, just waiting to be tried. Sure, you're going to try some that you don't like, some that you regret wasting your money on and some that simply aren't worth the alcohol units. But keep trying, whatever you do: there's bound to be something out there that will surprise and delight you if you keep on looking for it. Trust your taste. I've borrowed that slogan from one of my favourite wineries, Flagstone, but it is absolutely true. Maybe you didn't read all of this book; maybe you only dipped into it. There are no real twists in the tale, no exciting plot developments or raunchy sex scenes to finish up with. This book doesn't tell you everything about wine (sorry – no refunds), but, instead, it should give you the confidence to go out and find out about wine for yourself. So, trust your taste, have faith in your abilities and believe that there are lots of different wines out there that you might also enjoy.

◖◗ Talk to me. Unless you send me tweets about your amazing weight-loss products or emails telling me I've won the Nigerian lottery, I'm happy to chat online. You can find me @CathyMarston or via www.thewinecentre.co.za. Drop me a line and we can drink together in a virtual wine reality.

Cheers to that!

GLOSSARY OF WINE TERMS

Acidity. Very important part of all wines, but probably more crucial in whites and pinks than reds. Acidity stops a wine being flabby and boring, but too much can make it difficult to drink and create an unbalanced wine. Find out more in Chapter 6.

Balance. Probably the most important word in wine (apart from 'more'). A good wine is a balanced wine, where the acid, sweetness, fruit, tannin and oak all sit side by side in happy harmony. See Chapters 3 and 8 for more.

Black grape varieties. Lovely, deep-coloured, full-flavoured grapes with black skins producing red, white and rosé wines – yes really! See Chapter 14 for details of South Africa's favourites.

Brettanomyces. A strain of yeast that thrives in dirty cellars. If you like the smell of horseshit in your wine, choose one that is infected with 'brett'. Some people love it, others don't, but Chapter 12 will tell you more.

Corked wine. An infection called TCA (trichloroanisole) can get into wine, generally via an infected cork, and turn it bad. For details on how to deal with corked wine, see Chapter 12.

Fermentation. A chemical conversion process whose equation can be expressed as sugar + yeast = alcohol + CO_2. Fermentation is behind all alcohol and makes sense of a lot of stuff in this book – so it's quite important. Check out Chapter 2 for more details.

Lees. The yeast cells after they've done their job, eaten all the sugar, sunk to the bottom of the tank and died. Lees have lots of uses, particularly in the production of sparkling wines. See Chapter 15 for more.

Malolactic fermentation. A bacterial conversion of the tart, malic acids into softer, mellower acids. Takes place in all red wines and some whites. For more on its pros and cons, see Chapter 8.

Noble rot (or *Botrytis cinerea*). A glorious rot that affects certain grapes under certain special conditions, resulting in the finest sweet wines in the world. For details, see Chapter 17.

Oak. The only flavour that can be added to wine. Oak flavour is created in several different ways and it can impart lots of different flavours, depending on how old the oak is. It can also have a few other useful side effects. See Chapter 7 for all its wondrous guises.

Old vines. Vines become less productive as they get older (don't we all), but the fruit they produce is tastier and more interesting. See Chapter 11.

Oxidation or oxidised wine. The rotting process that starts to occur when fruit is exposed to oxygen. Wines become oxidised because they're made from fruit; it is generally to be avoided. See Chapters 7 and 12 for more information.

Preservatives in wine. Some wines can be kept for a long time because they contain natural preservation factors. See what they are in Chapter 13.

Pumping over or punching down. In winemaking, these are the two main methods used to keep the grapeskins mixed up in red wine so that the juice extracts all the necessary colour and tannin it needs. Chapter 10 gives you all the information you need.

Residual sugar. Also known as RS or just 'sweetness'; determines how sweet a wine is. Read more in Chapter 3.

Tannin. The mouth-puckering, cotton-wool-eating, dry sensation in your mouth after drinking some red wines is caused by tannin. Sounds dreadful – is it all bad? No, and Chapter 10 will tell you why.

Vintage. If all the grapes used to make the wine were grown and then picked in the same year, the winemaker can display that year on the bottle. More details in Chapter 16.

Volatile acidity. A fault that makes a wine smell of vinegar or nail-polish remover. Not nice, see Chapter 12 for details.

White grape varieties. In the same way as apples, there are lots of different types of white grapes. Find out more about South Africa's most popular ones in Chapter 9.

Yeast. No wine without yeast! Yeast triggers off the chemical conversion of sugar into alcohol. Yeast cells, or lees, also have an effect on wine after the yeast has died – particularly sparkling wine. See Chapters 2 and 15 for more.

Yield. Volume of grapes measured in tonnes that is harvested from one hectare of vineyards. Generally, the lower the yield, the higher the perceived quality of grapes. Chapter 11 will tell you more.

INDEX